INITIATING
SPIRITUAL
CONVERSATIONS

How to start them without being
pushy, weird, or 'religious'

Jeff Wilcox

CGM
costly grace media

Initiating Spiritual Conversations
How to start them without being pushy, weird, or 'religious'

Published by Costly Grace Media, Worthington, Ohio
www.costlygracemedia.com

Italics in biblical quotes indicate emphasis added.

All Scripture quotations are taken from: The Holy Bible: New International Version. Copyright © 1973, 1978, 1984 by International Bible Society. Used by permission of Zondervan Publishing House.

Book Design: Brian W. Gardner
Cover Design: David Schultz

ISBN: 978-0-9840335-2-2

This book is dedicated to Trilva, Chris (one and two), Katie and Everett – the most important people in my life.

table of contents

Acknowledgements

I would like to acknowledge the contributions of some of the people who have made this project much easier and, I'm sure, much more readable. I want to offer a special measure of thanks to my proofreaders: Barb Meade, Bill Johnston, John Hastings, and Bruce Robinson. Also, thank you to my publisher, Brian Gardner, who put up with a lot.

And finally, I want you to know that the names of the people mentioned in this book have not been changed. It's important to me that they know they've made a very valuable contribution to my life. And hopefully their stories will make an eternal impact on the lives of some people they will never meet this side of heaven.

INTRODUCTION

'Sharing your faith' is a little phrase that brings to mind many things. For some of us, it produces excitement and the prospect of playing a small role in helping to change someone's eternal destiny. For others, it brings back bad memories of pushy, self-righteous people trying to force their views on us. And for some of us, just the thought of sharing our faith produces feelings of dread and fear.

Whether you've been sharing your faith for a long time or you're just getting started, this book will give you some creative ways to increase your effectiveness in sharing the good news about Jesus Christ. Realizing that God has made each of us as unique individuals, I have included several creative ways of turning your conversations in a spiritual direction. Don't feel like you have to try to master, or even use, all of them. If you get a few ideas from this book that help you to become a more gracious and creative planter of spiritual seeds, then I will have accomplished my goal.

Here is a summary of what I have included in this book:

- We will begin with a short summary of the basics of the Christian faith
- Next, we will discuss some common reasons why many of us don't share our faith very often.

- Then, you will be given several very easy ways to bring up spiritual things in any ordinary conversation without being the least bit pushy, weird or 'religious'. You will discover various ways of bringing up and explaining the gospel that will not sound awkward (to you or to the other person).

- Finally, you will be given a list of principles (some of God's, followed by some of mine) that have really helped me in sharing my faith, including many phrases, questions and stories that I use all the time. And I will describe many real-life situations that you will find yourself in and some things that I typically say and do in those situations.

As you go through this book, you'll notice that I use the same phrases, stories and questions all the time. I do this because they all sound very normal and natural to me. But if you read one that you don't like, or that sounds awkward to you, then don't use it. Change it to something that sounds natural to you. The important thing here is that you embrace the principles. How you apply them depends on what's comfortable for you.

The Basics

Vince Lombardi used to start his spring practices by going back over the basics with his players. He would hold up a football in a room full of men who had spent most of their lives focusing on one and say, "Gentlemen, this is a football." It may seem pretty silly to us, but I'm going to do something similar here. I want to make sure that we're on the same page when I refer to things like salvation, the gospel and a personal relationship with Jesus.

The Bible clearly teaches that each of us is guilty of violating God's standards and that each of us owes him a debt that we could never pay. Jesus' death on the cross provides a way for God himself to pay that debt for us. But for that to happen, each of us must make a personal decision to believe that we are guilty and then we must choose to trust Jesus for that payment. Opening our hearts to Jesus, getting saved, receiving Christ and becoming a believer in Jesus are all phrases that mean the same thing. Making a decision to trust Jesus is what enables us to be forgiven, adopted into God's family and guaranteed a place in heaven when we die.

For people to be able to make this decision, a couple of things have to happen. First, God himself must open the eyes of their hearts so that they can understand the truth about themselves and about Jesus. How this happens is one of God's mysteries – one that we will never fully understand. The second thing that has to happen is that they have to somehow hear about God's offer.

Anyone can pick up a Bible and read the New Testament and be exposed to God's offer. But you and I both know that most people aren't going to do that. So, in order for them to hear about this good news, there has to be a messenger. God has decided that he is going to use us as his messengers to spread the good news. This book has been written to help you to become a more effective, gracious messenger for God.

But if you're not absolutely sure that you have personally chosen to trust Jesus and what he did on the cross, I urge you to do so. Tell God that you want a relationship with him, that you realize you're guilty before him, and that you want Jesus' death to apply to your life. Then, as God's adopted child, you can go out and share this good news with the people that you encounter every day.

Some of them will respond to the message and some won't. But if you use some of the creative ways in this book to initiate spiritual conversations, you will know that they have met at least one messenger who isn't pushy and self-righteous.

Finally, my prayer is that this book will help you to reach more people with the best news in the universe. Thank you for letting me share these things with you.

One

Barriers to Sharing our Faith

The ultimate reason that God wants us to share our faith is because he has decided that the gospel is going to be spread only through believers in Jesus. We do have a role to play in building God's church (Matthew 28:19,20; Romans 10:14), but who is doing the real building? Jesus said plainly that *he* is the one who will build his church (Matthew 16:18). When we realize that the power to do this comes not from us, but from God, a lot of our objections and barriers will seem rather lame.

But I'm afraid

Let's face it: for many of us it *is* scary to talk to people about spiritual things. There are a lot of reasons why many of us don't share our faith in Jesus very often and most of them seem to make perfect sense. As we discuss several, please know that I have felt (and given into) all of them many, many times. So don't think that because I wrote this book that I'm immune to these barriers, because I'm not.

We are often worried about what the other person will think of us if we bring up spiritual things. After all, who wants to be rejected and thought of as just another pushy, religious person? We may be worried that we will say the wrong thing and push that person even farther away from God. Our biggest barrier may be that we just don't know what to say or how to bring up spiritual things in a normal conversation without sounding like we just came out of left field. After all, we reason, who wants to feel like they've just been blindsided by something religious?

These are all valid reasons to not bring up our faith, but only if we forget whose message it really is. We didn't come up with the idea of personal guilt (Romans 3:23) and the offer of total forgiveness through trusting Jesus (Colossians 2:13,14; John 3:16). God did. He's the one who is actually drawing people toward himself (John 6:44). And God's Spirit is the one who is doing the real work of convicting people of the truth of the gospel (John 16:8). All he's calling on us to do is to be his messengers and to trust that he's the one supplying the open doors for us to share (Colossians 4:3). And he's the one who is supplying the real power of the gospel to impact people's hearts (Romans 1:16).

There are a lot of good books and DVDs on the topic of sharing your faith, and I have included a list of some of my favorite ones at the end of this book. I suspect that some of you have read one of my favorites: a book by Bill Fay entitled *Share Jesus Without Fear*. It's a great book, but my opinion is that he gave it the wrong title. It should have been called 'Share Jesus *In Spite Of Your* Fear' because I think that almost everyone reading this book is at least a little nervous about sharing their faith.

I teach a workshop on initiating spiritual conversations, and every time I do I feel two different emotions. First, I feel excitement. For me, there's nothing more fulfilling than helping someone become better equipped to share their faith. The second thing I always feel is nervousness. I have to consciously choose to show up and give my workshop, no matter how nervous I feel.

One of Jesus' most frequently given commands in the New Testament is 'don't be afraid' ("fear not"). Notice that Jesus didn't tell his followers not to *feel* afraid (because he knew that they would). He said that they shouldn't *be* afraid. Fear is simply a feeling; it's an emotion. We can't control what we feel, but we don't have to be controlled by our feelings. Every time I have a spiritual conversation with someone – every single time – I feel some fear.

I have had spiritual conversations with a lot of people and I still feel the same way every time. This isn't likely to go away for me, and it's not likely to go away for most of you. But hopefully, I'm going to give you some tools that will enable you to choose to speak up much more often in spite of the feelings that you will *probably* have.

After one of my workshops I was talking with a lady who's been a Christian for many years, and she told me that she had wanted to share her faith for a long time. But she always found herself very hesitant to do so. She said, "If the other person brings up spiritual things, I'll talk to them every time. But if they don't bring it up, I usually don't say anything, either." In other words, she was too afraid to even *try* to bring up spiritual things.

Is this where you are? Do you feel like it would be awkward for you to bring up spiritual things in the middle of a normal, everyday conversation? Are you afraid of what might happen (or not happen) if you try? If this is how you feel, you've come to the right place. I'm going to give you some really easy ways to bring up spiritual things *in any conversation* without being the least bit pushy or sounding out of place. And these are things you can do no matter how nervous you feel. If you start incorporating these things into your conversations with people, they will respond better than you ever thought possible. Your feelings of nervousness may never completely go away (mine haven't), but they will decrease. Just remember that God is only calling on us to be the messengers. The results of our conversations with people are completely between them and God.

But I'm not gifted

I'm sure that most of you are familiar with the concept of spiritual gifts, one of which is the gift of evangelism. Let's assume that you're convinced that God has not gifted you in the area of evangelism. And let's suppose that you're right – he hasn't. Will this prevent you from becoming a very effective sharer of your faith? Of course not – God wants each of us to be able to share what we know about him with others. My point here is this: effectively sharing your faith has nothing to do with gifting.

Oh sure, you can become more effective more quickly if you're gifted in this area. But everyone (including you) can become pretty effective in sharing their faith, no matter what personality and temperament one has. Remember this: gifting is *given* to us, but skill is *learned*.

I once read about a conversation that Michelangelo had with one of his admirers. The guy said that God had obviously given him a wonderful gift. Michelangelo replied, (paraphrase mine) "Yes, God has given me a great gift. But people would be shocked to know how many countless hours I spend working on that gift."

Now, do I have some gifting in the area of evangelism? I don't know; maybe I do. But there are two main
reasons that I have been able to share my faith pretty
often, neither of which has anything to do with gifting.
The first one is because I work at it. The second is that
I have trained myself to think in certain ways, which I
am going to share with you. These are two things that
everyone can do. And as you start turning the conversations *that you're already in* toward spiritual things, you'll
be amazed at how often you can plant spiritual seeds
with non-Christians. You'll also be amazed at how often
you'll be able to explain the gospel to people and have
them respond in a pretty positive way.

Always keep in mind that the only thing that has to
be present for us to share our faith is the willingness to
speak up. If we're willing to talk to people about spiritual things, then God will use us in some very surprising
ways. And the one thing that will consistently produce a
willing speaker is a grateful heart. In Isaiah chapter six,
God posed a question: "Whom shall I send? And who
will go for us?" Isaiah's answer is the one that God would
like to hear from each of us: "Here I am. Send me." But
notice what just preceded his answer: the assurance that
his guilt had been removed and his sins had been atoned
for. Isaiah's willingness to go and share God's message
was the result of his assurance of God's forgiveness.

Please take a few minutes at the beginning of your
day and remind yourself of how completely forgiven and
accepted you are because of what Jesus did on the cross.
The gratitude that this kind of thinking will produce is
very likely to result in more willingness on your part to

share spiritual truths with people. And the more often you
realize what's true of you solely because you're a believer
in Jesus, the more likely you will be to want others to
experience the same thing.

But I'm not good at relating to people

Before we get into the main part of the book, I'm
going to assume that a couple of things are true for you.
First, that you really do care about the people you're
talking with about spiritual matters. Second, that you
understand the importance of going out of your way to
show them that you care. If this is hard for you - if you're
not naturally a 'people person' - your first step is not to
just grit your teeth and go share the gospel with someone.
Your first step should be to pray. Ask God to give you a
heart for people – to see them the way he does. Ask him
to help you see them as lost, under his judgment and
in desperate need of what you have to share with them.

Then, step out and start serving some people, whether
you feel like it or not. If you do this, chances are that
your feelings toward others will change and you will
find yourself becoming a more caring person. And you'll
probably start seeing other people in a whole new light.
It's true that many of the people around us are lost and
under God's judgment. But don't ever forget that they're
also people that he created and that he loves very much.
Remember that your message will come across a whole
lot more clearly if the other person knows that you really
do care about them.

Like I said, there are a lot of good books and DVDs
out there on the subject of sharing your faith. And all of

the good ones have one thing in common: they focus a lot on listening to people and being genuinely interested in the things that interest them. In other words, we need to enter their world and let them know that what they believe and what they think are important to us, too. There's a trite little saying that's been around for a long time, but it's so true: people don't care how much you know until they know how much you care. So start finding ways to let people know you care about them. This is how you earn the right to be heard.

I wrote this book with a very specific purpose in mind: to give you some tools that will enable you to develop confidence in bringing up spiritual issues. Because when you're able to take a conversation and turn it in a spiritual direction in a very natural way, then when you do ask spiritual questions and make statements about Jesus, it doesn't come across as pushy or weird or out of left field. Doing this will remove much of the fear on your part and it will lower the stress level on *their* part. These are the two most common components of spiritual conversations: fear for you and stress for them.

Once you're able to turn a normal conversation in a spiritual direction, then you can use any approach you feel comfortable with when you discuss spiritual things. And I will share with you a few that I find helpful. But the key to this whole process is only discussing spiritual things *after* they have been brought into the conversation. Again, the last thing we ever want to do is to have the other person feel like they have just been blindsided by something religious that just came out of nowhere.

Notice that there are two separate components of this process. The first is turning the conversation in a spiritual direction. The second is actually discussing spiritual issues and, hopefully, explaining the gospel. And I'm going to talk about both.

But what if they won't listen?

Let's say that you read this book and decide that you're going to go out and start having more spiritual conversations with people. And suppose the first ten people you try to talk to are completely uninterested. Here are some of the thoughts that are going to go through your mind:

- I really tried but, just like I thought, I am not cut out for this.
- Apparently, people aren't nearly as open as this guy said they are.
- All I'm doing here is pushing these people farther away from God. And that's the last thing I want to do.

Now, how do I know what you're going to think - is it because I'm omniscient? No, it's because I've been there. When these thoughts come, *and they will*, don't believe them, because they are *not* true. Yes, you are going to run into a lot of spiritually closed people, but that fact shouldn't change what we do at all. Because if you plant seeds with people, especially if you do it in a loving and gracious way, God *will* use them in some way in their lives, even when you don't think that's ever going to be possible.

But what if I blow it?

In addition to running into a lot of closed people, you are going to make a lot of mistakes, but I urge you to learn from those mistakes and keep trying. I want you to know that, even after many years of sharing my faith, I blow it on a regular basis. Far too often I talk when I should be listening. Far too often I jump in with a response before I really understand what the other person is saying. But I keep trying. And that's what God wants you to do. What's important to God isn't our ability – it's our availability and our willingness.

I heard a little saying a long time ago that we should all keep in mind: more people would consider becoming Christians if they could meet some people who know Jesus, but who are otherwise fairly normal. I think this is a huge part of our job – to be able to be that non-pushy, non-weird, non-religious person. I'm sure that some of you don't share your faith very often because someone in your past was real pushy with you. They may have had the message right, but the way they did it really turned you off, didn't it? And you're so afraid of doing that to someone else that you don't say anything at all.

That's a real valid concern; the last thing we want to do is to push someone farther away from God. But consider this: you *did* become a Christian, didn't you? You made that decision in spite of your bad experiences. Which means that there was probably at least one person in your past that did share their faith with you in a sensitive way. And you can be that sensitive person for someone else, too. Always remember that the message will come across much better if people see the messenger as fairly normal.

Is this all up to me?

Since it's up to us to choose to talk to people and to share the good news with them, it's real easy to believe that it's up to us to convince them of the truth. And we may be tempted to overlook God's role in this whole process, which is to draw people toward himself. This is a mystery that we'll never understand in this life. Don't ever forget that God is the one who's doing the real work in people's hearts. And it's the Holy Spirit who is convicting them of their guilt and their need to trust Jesus.

We can inform and persuade and sometimes even beg people to respond to God's offer. Yes, on a rare occasion begging is appropriate, as Paul says in 2 Corinthians 5:20. And a bit later, I'll share with you a time that I did just that. But it's not our cleverness or our creativity that are most important when sharing our faith. It's the truth of our message and the power of God to impact people with that truth that will ultimately determine how effective we are.

But we do have a role in this process and it's very significant; but it's also minor. God is the one who saves people; we're just the messengers. Our role is to share spiritual truths with people in a loving, gracious way and to help them understand what God's offer through Jesus really is. Most of the people you talk to have some kind of church background and almost everyone has heard about Jesus, but many of them have never had the gospel explained in a way that they can understand. So don't make the mistake of assuming that people with a long church background don't need to hear the gospel, because a lot of them really do.

There's another very significant role that we can play: we can pray for people. I suggest that you start a written list of the folks that you have planted (or are going to plant) seeds with and pray for them on a regular basis. Always remember that talking to God about that person is just as important as talking to them about God.

I have a good friend who is a very dedicated sharer of his faith and he often texts me, and several other people, asking for prayer for someone he has just planted a seed with. I do the same with him and we have both been quite surprised at the answers to those prayers. I suggest that you find several friends who are also trying to share their faith and be each other's prayer partners. You can simply share the first name of the person you had a spiritual conversation with and ask for prayer for them. I guarantee that more fruit will come from your efforts if they are accompanied by more prayer.

Two

Context is King

This book is all about having spiritual conversations with people. Most of us know how to have a conversation with another person – we do it all the time. But the key here for us is the term 'spiritual'. How can we get spiritual things onto the table without the other person feeling like they have just been blindsided by something religious? Well, the key to doing this is found in a single word: *context*. Spiritual things don't sound awkward *only* if they're brought up in *context*.

Let me give you an illustration. Suppose that you're on a plane: the plane takes off, you get settled into your seat and you start chatting with the person seated next to you. Assume that, like in many normal conversations, both of you share a bit about your families and you find out that the other person has children at home. At this point, it would be very normal for you to ask the other person "How old are your kids?"

Now, suppose you get to your destination and you're walking through the airport and a person you have never seen before approaches you. Suppose they walk right up to you, look you in the eye and their very first words are: "How old are your children?" You'll probably feel like running away from them, right? At the very least, they will come across as very weird. Now, why does this question sound so normal on the plane and so weird at the airport? Because on the plane, it's asked in context.

Here's a good example of bringing up spiritual things in context. Several years ago, I met a friend for dinner and he had brought along a friend of his that I had never met. We chatted for a while and I found out that he was a huge football fan. The Super Bowl had just been played and Tom Brady was named the MVP. I asked him if he had seen the interview with Tom Brady shortly after the game, and he said that he had.

I told him that I had just seen a couple of minutes of it, but it was the part where Tom Brady said, in essence, that he had everything anyone could ever want – fame, fortune and a Super Bowl ring. Then he said that he couldn't help but wonder if there wasn't much more to life than that. At that point I said to the guy I was talking to, "Boy, that sure sounds like a spiritual statement to me. What do you think?" He readily agreed and we went on to have a great spiritual conversation.

I can assure you from many years of experience, that if you bring up spiritual things in context, it will not sound weird or out of place. And the vast majority of the time, the other person will not react in a negative way. You will be very surprised at how many of the negative things you were so afraid would happen never do. And any time you're with another person, in the same place for the same reason, you have a lot in common with them and you have a very natural opening for a spiritual conversation.

For example, suppose you're on a plane again. You and the person sitting beside you already have a great deal in common. You're both going somewhere, you've both come from somewhere, you both have a reason for your trip and you probably both live somewhere and have families. So, questions like "Where are you headed today?" "Is this a business trip or for pleasure?", "What do you do for a living?" all sound very normal in this context.

What are the best questions to ask?

Something that I consciously do is to ask *open-ended questions* – ones that can't be easily answered 'yes' or 'no'. You will get so much more information from someone with an open-ended question. For example, instead of asking "Do you have any hobbies?" ask, "What are your hobbies?" or "How do you spend your free time?" Instead of asking "Are you a sports fan?" ask, "What sports do you follow?" And instead of asking someone "Did you grow up going to a church?" ask, "What's *your* church background?"

This is one of my favorite questions and I always ask it at some point. Now, I don't always ask this question during the first conversation I have with someone. It may be much later – after I've gotten to know them a bit. And I only ask this question *after spiritual things have been brought up in the conversation*. If this is one of your very first questions, you are going to come across as pretty weird.

You may have read Bill Fay's book *Share Jesus Without Fear* that I mentioned earlier. The approach that he takes with people is to ask them a series of questions. He then has the person read some verses from the Bible and he asks them what they mean. It's a great way to share biblical truths with people. But once again, turning the conversation in a spiritual direction *before* you bring these things up will enable you to sound like you're not coming out of left field.

The church I attend has several free health clinics for underprivileged people every week. At the beginning of each clinic, while the patients are waiting to see the nurses and doctors, they are all told that the clinic is run by a local church. And they are told that many of the volunteers who will be helping to serve them have a personal relationship with Jesus. Spiritual things are already on the table, so when our folks ask spiritual questions and offer to pray with anyone who has a need, it sounds very natural. Again, it's because all of this is done in context.

How do I do this without sounding weird?

At this point, you're probably wondering how you can ask a question about someone's church background in the middle of a normal, everyday conversation without sounding like you just came out of nowhere. So, I'm going to give you a couple of ways that I typically do it.

Once you get to know a person a bit, it's very likely that you can come up with someone you go to church with who has some things in common with the other person. For example, once you find out what the other person does for a living, chances are good that you know someone at your church who works in the same field. Then you can mention your friend and, at some point, say that you go to the same church. And I always use the same phrase: "We go to the same non-denominational church in the north end of town." Then, when you ask about *their* church background, it will come across as very normal. Following are a couple of examples of how this can be done in a very natural way.

I live in Columbus, Ohio, the home of The Ohio State University, where every other person is a very dedicated (rabid, actually) football fan. There have been many times during a conversation with one of them that the OSU Buckeye football team has come up. I will say that I have a friend named Charlie who was a photographer for the local newspaper for many years and that he took some of the most famous pictures of former coach Woody Hayes on the sidelines during a game. He even gave me two signed prints of pictures that he had taken, which I have hanging in my office. I will go on to say what a great guy he is and that I met him several years ago at this "church in the north end" that we both attend. That sounds very normal, doesn't it? Why? Because it was brought up in context.

Suppose I'm talking to someone who is a computer expert and who works in the IT field. I will tell them about another friend of mine (also named Charlie) that I meet for breakfast almost every week. Often I will say, "My friend, Charlie, is a real geek – he writes *computer code* for a living. And every so often, I'll make the big mistake of asking him what he's working on at the office – and he will actually tell me. And then, for the next few minutes, all I can do is pretend to be interested (and nod and smile knowingly), not understanding *anything* he says. Charlie's a good friend and I've known him for many years. I originally met him at 'this church I go to in the north end." Again, this doesn't sound the least bit out of place, because it perfectly fits the context of the conversation.

Do you see how natural this sounds? It's not the least bit pushy or awkward. Best of all, the other person doesn't feel like you've just come completely out of left field. It sounds normal because it's done in the context of a normal, everyday conversation. Here is a very natural place for you to ask about their church background. You might say this: "Speaking of church, I'm curious. What's *your* church background?" Or, you might say this: "I hope you don't mind, but I'm curious. What's your church background?"

And if you're talking with a person that you know, someone that you have already had several non-spiritual conversations with, you could put it this way: "You know, I don't think church has ever come up before in one of our conversations. But I'm curious. What's *your* church background?" Wouldn't you agree that this sounds very normal and natural? Again, *context* is the key.

Building on their church background

Once I find out what their church background is, I usually ask another question: "Do you still go there?" This question can give you an awful lot of information about where that person is spiritually. If they say they don't go there any more, the way they say it can be very revealing.

If they say, "No, I know I should, but I don't", you can simply ask them why - and they will probably tell you. If they say they don't go anymore and are real emphatic about it, you can say something like this: "Sounds like you didn't have very good experiences there. What was it that turned you off so much about that place?" And they'll probably tell you that, too.

So, now you know what their church background is,

whether or not they still go there and maybe what kind of experiences they had. And at some point, you can relate a story about yourself or someone you know who has a similar church background. If their church background matches yours, you can tell them a bit about your experiences in that church. If their background doesn't match yours, you can bring up a friend (or even the friend of a friend) who went to the same kind of place they did and tell a story about what they remember about their experiences.

I personally know someone who grew up in most of the major denominations, and you probably do, too. But if you can't think of any, start asking your friends who are believers in Jesus. Ask them what it was like going to their church. Also ask them if they heard the gospel taught there. You're going to be shocked at how many of your friends grew up going to a church, but who never had the gospel taught or explained to them at their church. And don't assume that a person who grew up going to church is a Christian, because many of them aren't and they need to have the gospel explained to them just as much as anyone.

There's another answer that you might get to the church background question. They may say that they don't have one at all – that they never went to church. When someone tells me this, I always say, "Boy, are you lucky." Then, when they ask what I mean, I say, "Just think of all the wrong stuff you don't have to unlearn." And they usually laugh.

Suppose the other person reacts very negatively to your question about their church background and they

say one of the following: "I don't want to talk about religion!" or "I never talk about religion," or "That's none
of your business!" If this happens, don't panic. Instead
simply ask, "Why do you feel that way?" They may just
tell you. And if they do, you will know a *lot* about where
they are spiritually.

If they ask you why you want to know about their
church background, you can simply repeat that you're
just curious. But if they don't want to talk about it past
this point, just let it go. If you pursue it any further,
you'll probably come across as just another one of those
pushy, religious people. But that doesn't mean that you
can never bring up spiritual things with them again. You
can always let some time go by and go back to them and
say, "I remember you saying that you don't want to talk
about spiritual things. Do you still feel that way?" Or,
you could say, "I remember you saying that you don't
want to talk about spiritual things. I'll bet you have real
good reasons for feeling that way. What are they?" And
they just might tell you.

As I said before, most of the time you are not going to
get a hostile response to your church background question and you can continue the conversation. But I'm sure
that for some of you, this has not been your experience.
If you frequently get a negative response when you try
to bring up spiritual things, I suggest you review your
approach. You'll probably find that you brought up spiritual things without considering how it was going to sound
to the other person. Just remember to always consider the
context of the situation you're in. And again, the more
information you have about where they are spiritually,

the better equipped you are to discuss spiritual things with them.

Another question I often ask is this: "How about your family - do they still go there?" If this person's family has been going to the same church for many years, keep in mind that family loyalty to a church or a denomination can be very strong. And a lot of people are very hesitant to even *consider* something different from what their church teaches (and what their entire family believes) - even if what they're hearing from you is true.

Let's say that you're talking to a person who's been going to the same church all of his or her life and they don't hear the gospel taught there. When you bring up a personal decision to trust Jesus, this may sound very foreign to them. They may actually be afraid to even consider it because they may feel that they would be betraying their family. So if it's obvious that they're feeling this way, you can say something like this: "I'm not suggesting that you leave the (Catholic, Presbyterian, Methodist, etc.) church. Far from it." And that's not the real issue at all, is it? The real issue is whether or not this person knows Jesus personally. And if they don't think you're trying to pull them away from their church or their family (or their culture), they may relax enough to actually hear what you're saying.

Here is a short review of the steps that I take:

1. Ask open-ended questions to find out some things about that person that are important to them
2. Come up with someone at your church who has some things in common with them
3. Mention that you both go to the same church
4. Ask about their church background
5. Find out if they still go there
6. Ask about their experiences in that church

Three

Explaining the Gospel

Using their church background

I would like to share with you a couple of ways that I bring the gospel into the conversation. One of the main ways I do this is by using their church background. For example, when talking with someone who has a very formal church background, I may say:

> "I know that the _____ church teaches a lot of good things. And they talk about Jesus and his death on the cross to pay for sins. But how often does your pastor (or minister or priest) talk about a *personal* relationship with God through personal faith in Jesus?"

Now, suppose the person I'm talking with grew up going to the same kind of church that I attended for several years when I first moved to Ohio. I will say,

> "You know, I went to a _____ church, like you did, for three years when I first moved here. And one thing that I clearly remember about that church is that I never heard someone in the pulpit talk about personal salvation. You know – making a personal decision to trust Jesus. How did they present that in *your* church?"

Or, I can mention a friend who grew up in the same kind of church they did and say the same thing.

"My friend grew up going to a _____ church, too, and they told me that they don't remember ever hearing their pastor (minister, priest) talk about personal salvation. You know – making a personal decision to trust Jesus. How did they present that in your church?"

I have done this countless times and I have never had a hostile response to these questions. I'm certain that it's because it's always done in context and doesn't sound like it just came out of nowhere. Oh sure, I've had conversations with a lot of people who didn't want to talk about spiritual things. But if these questions are asked in a gracious way, and in context, they don't sound awkward to people at all.

Using the word 'gospel'

Even when the concept of a personal relationship with Jesus is out on the table, many people don't understand what it means. So we need to be able to explain it in a way that they can really relate to. One way I commonly explain the gospel is to ask, "You've heard the word 'gospel' before, right?" And they will almost always say that they have. Then, I will say, "Well, it sounds like a religious word, but it actually means 'good news'. And you can't have good news without what?" They will usually finish the sentence for you with "bad news."

Then, I go on and say,

"It's kind of like the justice system in this country. When someone breaks the law and is sent to prison, we say that they're paying their debt to society, right? That violation of the law creates a real debt that has to be paid. In the same way, we each owe God a real debt that someone has to pay. That's the bad news.

And that's where Jesus comes in. His death on the cross can pay the real debt we each owe to God so that he won't have to judge us when we die. We get complete forgiveness by personally trusting Jesus and the payment that he made. And that's why it's called 'good news'."

I have a friend, a dear lady who is in her mid-nineties, who lives in a nursing home. Several years ago we were talking, and I found out that she had spent her entire life in a formal church and was, in her own words, "actively looking for the truth." But like so many people, she had heard of Jesus' death on the cross hundreds of times, but she had never had anyone explain Jesus' offer in a way she could understand. When I used the explanation of the word 'gospel', the light came on for her and she made the decision to trust Jesus immediately.

Using an adoption analogy

Many times, I have used the following explanation with people.

"Becoming a believer in Jesus is actually a change of identity. There's a big difference between just being one of God's creations and actually being in his family. And here's what I mean: Have you ever heard the saying 'we're all God's children'? Well, that isn't *technically* true. We *are* his creations, but we're not his children until we personally come into his family."

"We can't relate to God as his children because there's a huge barrier between us and him – our violations of his moral standards. In other words, what separates us from him is our sins. But when we make the decision to trust Jesus personally, God himself removes this barrier and we get adopted into his family. And once this happens, God doesn't see us as guilty and alienated from him any more – he sees us as his own son or daughter."

Both of these ways of explaining the gospel are very biblical, aren't they? And they both contain the two basic elements of what the gospel really is. The first element is that we are all guilty before God (Romans 3:23) and that the penalty for that guilt is spiritual death (Romans 6:23) The second is that personal faith in Jesus and his death on the cross will take care of that problem forever (John 1:12; John 3:16; Romans 6:23; Romans 10:9, 10). It's that simple, folks. And when we explain these things in a gracious way, people really do start to have a much better understanding of the decision that they need to make.

FOUR

USING WORD PICTURES

One of my favorite ways of explaining the gospel is by using word pictures. This was one of Jesus' favorite ways of explaining spiritual truths to people, too. If you go back and read the gospels, you will see how often Jesus did this himself. Much of the time, he used an illustration that the other person could really relate to. Now, what do we call the illustrations that Jesus often used? They're called parables. And what is a parable? It's simply a word picture that illustrates a spiritual truth.

I can tell you, from many years of experience, that when you explain the gospel in ways that people can relate to (ways that are biblical), they start to understand God's offer much more clearly. Here is the way I typically use them.

Once the conversation is going in a spiritual direction, something will almost always come up that perfectly fits a word picture. Here is how I bring them into the conversation. I will say to the person "You're familiar with parables, right – the little word pictures Jesus used when he taught?" And they will almost always say that they are. "I heard a great word picture along these lines that really made sense to me. Let me run it by you and see what you think." And they will always let you. So I'm going to give you a few situations where using word pictures might be very effective.

Several times, I have heard someone say something like this: "I've always been a Christian" or "I've always believed in Jesus." Now you and I know that isn't true – no one is *born* believing in Jesus. But don't jump in and correct them. They probably *do* believe a lot of facts about Jesus. And they probably *do* believe that Jesus was a real person who actually died on a cross. In other words, they may know quite a bit *about* Jesus, but they may not know him personally.

So, in response to what they said, I would simply say "I'm real glad" or "That's great." Then, I would say, "You're familiar with parables, right – the little word pictures Jesus used when he taught? I heard a great one along these lines that really made sense to me. Let me run it by you and see what you think" The word picture I would use with this person is about knowing the President.

Do you believe in the President?

"Let me ask you a question - do you believe in the President?" Then, I stop and say

"Now, wait a minute - if you don't like the current one, you can go back to the previous one. What I'm really asking is this: do you believe that he really exists? OK, do you know what he looks like? Do you know what his wife looks like? Do you know what his voice sounds like? Do you know where he lives – that big white house on Pennsylvania Avenue? So, you know a lot about him, right? But could you have breakfast with him tomorrow?"

At this point, they may look at you like you're crazy and they will say something like "Of course not." Then, simply ask them "Why not?" And they will always give you a logical reason why you can't just waltz into the presence of the President. And no matter what reason they give, you can continue to ask the "why?" question. One of the best responses I have ever gotten was "Because the Secret Service won't let me." This sounds very logical and true, right? So I simply said, '*Why* won't the Secret Service let you?" He thought for a moment and said, "Well, because I'm not on the approved list." To which I replied "*Why* aren't you on the approved list?"

Eventually, he got around to the right reason and said something like, "I guess because he doesn't know me." Then I said that it's the same way with Jesus. We can know a lot *about* him and still not know him personally. And this is where the decision to trust him comes in.

I guarantee that you will run into people who have had some negative experiences with Christians. We need to realize that a lot of people got their negative perceptions of Jesus from some of his followers who were being very poor ambassadors for him. So, when you hear negative comments, don't get defensive (which is what I used to do). Simply say something like this: "I don't blame you at all for feeling that way. Those people really turn me off, too, and I don't want to be around them, either." I can honestly say that and I assume that you probably can, too.

A foreign ambassador

Then, you could say "You're familiar with parables, right...?" Then I would use a word picture of an ambassador coming to this country representing a foreign government.

> "Suppose an ambassador was sent here to represent a foreign government and suppose he acted like a total jerk. Now, because of his behavior, we would be justified in rejecting that person, right? But it would be a big mistake to write off the entire government that sent him, wouldn't it? Instead, we should just assume that he was being a very poor representative. It's the same way with Jesus. Unfortunately, he has some representatives out there giving him a real bad name, but that doesn't mean that he isn't worth getting to know."

How about if someone says this to you: "The God I believe in would never judge anyone," or "I could never believe in a God who would send people to hell." Once again, it wouldn't be helpful to get defensive and have an argument with them. Instead, a good response would be: "You know, that makes a lot of sense." Because to the average non-Christian, this *does* make a lot of sense. And if you remember back before you were a believer in Jesus, it probably made a lot of sense to you, too.

Being found guilty in court

You could simply respond this way: "Tell me something. Do you believe that God is going to be perfectly fair with everyone?" They will probably say that they do. Then, you could say, "You're familiar with parables, right...?" And you could use a word picture of being in court that goes something like this.

"Suppose you're in court for breaking the law and the evidence is overwhelming that you're guilty. They even have a video of you doing it. And let's further suppose that you think the particular law that you broke is ridiculous and petty and shouldn't even *be* a law and that what you did wasn't really a big deal. That probably wouldn't matter much to the court, would it?"

"Let's further suppose that the judge is actually your father. Now, the judge has a big problem. He's your father and he loves you and would never want to see you go to prison – for any reason. But as the judge, he's compelled to uphold the law. So to be really fair, after hearing all of the evidence, he would have to pronounce you guilty, right?"

"Now, suppose the judge offers to serve your sentence for you because he loves you. Justice would still be served. Someone would pay for that crime, but it wouldn't be you. So, you're absolutely right. God *is* very loving, but he's also totally fair and that's where Jesus comes in. Jesus offers to pay the debt that we owe so that God doesn't *have* to judge us when we die."

Here's another good situation for a word picture: let's say that you've just said to the person you're talking to, "You've heard the word 'gospel', right?" And you get to the point where you describe the bad news (our guilt) and you say "I don't know about you, but I know I'm guilty." Now, instead of agreeing with you, suppose they say something like this: "Well, nobody's perfect. Sure, I've done some things wrong. Everybody has. But I believe in God – I think he'll honor that."

Well, once again, don't jump in and correct them and start an argument. Instead, say, "I'm glad you believe in God." And then you can say, "You know what parables are, right…?" Here are a couple of word pictures that would come in real handy in this situation.

In debt for ten million dollars

"Suppose you had started a .com company back in the early nineties and had made a fortune, like many people did. But suppose that a series of bad business decisions resulted in you losing it all, and you were left with a ten million dollar debt to the IRS (which is very possible, considering the money some of those people made). You're hopelessly in debt, you can't bankrupt out of it and you can't even begin to pay the interest on it. Now, suppose one of your former business partners hears about your plight and sends you a personal check for ten million dollars."

"You can take that check home, hold it in your hand, and believe with all your heart that it's genuine. You can *absolutely believe* that it has the ability to completely solve your problem and give your life back to you. But for that check to do you any good, what would you have to do with it? You would have to cash it, right?"

Diagnosed with terminal cancer

"Or suppose that you have just been diagnosed with stage four pancreatic cancer and you've been given a few months to live. So, you get several more opinions and all of the specialists concur – you're going to die soon. Now, let's suppose that you're a big Facebook fan and you post something very general about being sick and that you would like to connect with some of your old friends in person."

"And suppose one of your best friends from high school calls you the next day and says he's going to be in your town for the weekend and wants to get together with you. So you meet for dinner, he asks what's going on, and you tell him. Imagine him looking at you and saying, "Yeah, I assumed it was something bad. I'm going to share something with you that you can never repeat."

"I started a huge pharmaceutical company and we're in the process of clinical trials with the FDA of a drug that will completely cure your cancer." Then, he gives you a vial containing a single capsule and tells you that he guarantees it will cure you. Now, you can take it home, hold it in your hand and *really believe* that it will work. But for it to do you any good, what would you have to do? You'd have to take the pill, right?"

"In both of these cases, belief wouldn't help much without an action on your part. So I agree with you that believing in God is a wonderful thing and is essential. But getting our sins forgiven involves coming to God *his way* and making a decision to trust Jesus."

I'm a pretty good person

I hear all the time, and you will, too, things like these: "Well, nobody's perfect," or "All we can do is try to do our best," or "I always try to do the right thing," or "I haven't done anything terrible – certainly not anything bad enough for God to judge me."

These statements usually mean that the person feels that they've lived a pretty good life. So a good response would be to say: "What I think you're saying is that you've lived a pretty good life, right?" If they agree, please don't jump in and correct them. A much better thing to say would be: "Well, using human standards, I'm sure you *have* lived a pretty good life. Using human standards, most of us have lived pretty good lives" And then, you can say, "You're familiar with parables, right...?" And here's one that I have used many times.

"I have a friend who attended college in California and he and his buddies used to go out to the pier and play a game they called 'jumping to Catalina.' Now, Catalina Island is twenty-two miles off the coast. They would take turns running as fast as they could and leaping off the pier. Some of them were very athletic and made very good jumps, while others barely fell off the end of the pier. Some of them were far better athletes than the others and got much closer to Catalina Island than their buddies."

"But the standard wasn't just being better than the next guy – the standard was reaching Catalina Island. And who even came close to doing that? It's the same way with God. No matter how good we look next to other people, we fall impossibly short of his standards."

FIVE

GOD'S PRINCIPLES

I want to share with you some of the general principles that have been invaluable to me in sharing spiritual things with people. But first, I think it's appropriate to look at some of God's principles. The best summary in the Bible of how God wants us to interact with people as we share the good news is Colossians 4:3-6:

> "And pray for us, too, that God may open a door for our message, so that we may proclaim the mystery of Christ, for which I am in chains. Pray that I may proclaim it clearly, as I should. Be wise in the way you act toward outsiders; make the most of every opportunity. Let your conversation be always full of grace, seasoned with salt, so that you may know how to answer everyone." (Colossians 4:3–6)

Let me ask you a question: who wrote the book of Colossians? Paul did. And who inspired him to write it? Obviously, God did. So this passage is actually God telling us how he wants us to approach people as we share the good news of Jesus.

I have included these passages on one of the pages in the back of this book. I would suggest that you cut the page out and tape it onto your bathroom mirror. Then every morning, as you gaze at that incredibly attractive person standing in front of you, take a minute and read these verses. If you do this, I guarantee that your day will be different.

Pray for open doors

We need to ask God to work behind the scenes – to supernaturally arrange for us to be in circumstances that are conducive to spiritual conversations. The more we ask God to do this, the more doors he will open for us. And the more often we ask, the more often we will be reminded to look for these open doors. Because they are there.

We also need to pray for people who are receptive to the gospel message. God arranges for people who are open to his offer to come into our lives. These divine appointments are one of God's specialties.

Now, how are we going to know if a person is receptive to spiritual things? We have to talk to them and find out. So we also need to pray and ask God to give us the desire and the willingness to speak up and talk to people.

Do you do these things on a regular basis? Do you pray for God to bring open people into your life? And do you ask him to motivate you to speak up? You'll be amazed at how often God answers prayers like these.

Proclaim the gospel clearly

When Paul and Peter went into a new area to share the good news about Jesus, they didn't just hand out leaflets and wait for people to ask them questions. And they didn't just build a church building and wait for curious people to show up. They reasoned with people. In other words, they had a dialogue. When we're talking with people, there are a lot of things we can do to adorn our message – things like loving them and serving them and letting them know we really care about them. And those things are critically important. But there is no substitute for explaining the gospel to people verbally.

Can you do this? Can you give a short presentation of the gospel that's easily understood? It doesn't have to be long or real complicated. In chapter 4, I gave you several ways that I routinely explain the gospel that sound very natural to me. Feel free to use them or adapt them to fit your particular style of conversation. What's important is that you explain the good news in very simple terms that anyone can understand. Just make sure that the other person clearly hears two things: 1. We're all guilty and deserve God's judgment and 2. Jesus can pay that debt for us if we will only choose to trust him.

And when you get to the point in your conversations where you can explain the gospel, don't forget that your own personal experience can make a huge impact on the other person. What your life was like before you came to know Jesus compared to what it's like now is a very powerful thing to share.

Use wisdom when dealing with non-Christians

If we treat people like projects, or if we're self-righteous, arrogant, or pushy, we are not going to be very effective in sharing our faith in Jesus. This is true even if our message is technically correct. If you've ever had one of those weird, pushy people talk to you about Jesus, you know exactly what I mean.

Take advantage of the opportunities that God gives you

When you do have an opportunity – when you're in a situation where you could very easily have a spiritual conversation with someone – choose to speak up and talk to them. Make no mistake: most of the time, you will have to make a conscious choice to do this in spite of the nervousness you will probably feel.

Be gracious to the people you interact with

Go out of your way to treat them like they're people that God loves, people that Jesus died for, because that's exactly who they are. Don't be argumentative and don't be too anxious to point out that their worldview is wrong. We want so badly for people to hear the truth that it's real easy to fall into the habit of being way too quick to correct them.

Be prepared and willing to answer people's questions

One of the main reasons that many of us spend so much time studying the Bible is so that we can know what it really says. I heard a real good analogy of knowing the Bible well. People who study the Bible are very similar to the people in the Treasury Department who deal with counterfeit money. Those folks spend an awful lot of time studying real money. They know real money so well that when the counterfeit does come along, it's very easy to spot. We need to do the same thing with the Bible.

1 Peter 3:15 puts it this way: "always being ready to make a defense to everyone who asks you to give an account for the hope that is in you, yet with gentleness

and reverence." Notice that Peter says to give a defense – not to get defensive; there's a huge difference. We need to be able to give people reasons for why we believe what we believe.

Can you do this? Can you give people some reasons why you believe that the Bible is actually true, as opposed to the book of Mormon or the writings of the eastern religions? We need to be able to do this because a lot of people want some evidence before they make a major decision like becoming a believer in Jesus. If you're not sure you can do this, read a book or two on the subject of the reliability of the Bible - there are a lot of really good ones available.

You are going to be asked questions that you can't answer and it happens to me, too (on a pretty regular basis). And a lot of people don't share their faith very often because they're afraid they won't be able to answer someone's questions. One of the most common misconceptions is that we're disqualified from sharing our faith if we don't know enough about the Bible. Maybe this is your main stumbling block. Do you think that you have to be a Bible scholar in order to be effective in sharing your faith? Well, looking back at the beginning of the church shows that this just isn't true. How many of Jesus' early followers were New Testament scholars? (Hint: none, because they didn't have the New Testament).

A lady came up to me after one of my workshops and told me that this had been the biggest barrier to sharing her faith. She felt that since she didn't know the location of all of the important verses, she couldn't be effective. Then she said to me, "But now I realize that, although

I may not know chapter and verse, I do know the truth." That realization gave her the freedom and the motivation to go out and share that truth a lot more often. Hopefully, it will do the same thing for you.

Six

General Principles

Now, I want to give you some general principles that have been very helpful to me. Please keep in mind that these principles are not just impersonal formulas. They're not just things we can use to manipulate people into believing what we believe. They are simply tools that we can use to share the good news about Jesus with the people we interact with every day.

Changing our thinking

One of the critical keys to becoming effective in sharing our faith is to change some of our thinking. The primary change that many of us need to make is to resist the thought that no one is interested in spiritual things. I know that way too often our thinking goes something like this: "I'm sure he (or she) wouldn't be interested in hearing about anything spiritual from me." Does this sound familiar? I want to share a little story that illustrates just how wrong that kind of thinking can be.

I have a friend named Brad who used to be a pretty dedicated sharer of his faith. But over the years, he let himself get distracted in various ways and he even got to the point where he was convinced that no one wanted to hear about spiritual things – especially from him. This had completely neutralized him from sharing anything spiritual with anyone. But after several years of being in this state, he realized that he needed to start talking to people again.

He was on a business trip and was in a taxi in Milwau-
kee and decided that he just had to say something to the
driver. So he looked at the guy in the mirror and asked
if he could ask him a question. The driver looked back at
him and said, "Yeah – I guess so." My friend then blurted
out (completely out of left field), "If you died today, do
you know where you would spend eternity?"

Now, keep in mind that this is a cab driver in Milwau-
kee. And he probably thought to himself, "Uh oh – why
does this guy want to know about when I die? Am I in
big trouble here?" But once the driver realized that my
friend wasn't going to do him in, they went on to have
a great spiritual conversation. The driver even gave my
friend his cell phone number and said, "If you're ever
back in town, call me and we can continue this conversation." So we should assume that people *do* want to talk
about spiritual things, because a lot of them really do.
We should also assume that people *don't* want to talk
about spiritual things with someone who is pushy and
uptight – so don't be one.

Provide a safe environment

If people are going to share what they really believe
with you, they have to feel like it's safe to do so. We need
to provide an environment that is comfortable for them.
People need a place where they're not lectured or looked
down on for their beliefs – a place where they're treated
with respect. I personally think that this is why a lot of
people avoid churches and the people who go there – they
don't see religious people as a safe place to discuss what

they really believe. And unfortunately, they're often right.

Be genuinely interested

Before we try to *tell* people things, we need to spend time just *listening* to them. People need to know that we really are interested in what they think and believe. If we will take the time to find out where they're coming from, they will be much more receptive to letting us share with them what we believe.

Here is an example of being genuinely interested: many years ago, I was in Florida with my wife at a frozen yogurt store. When we came out, we noticed a Christian Science reading room right next door, complete with a smiling older lady at a reception desk. I told my wife that I was going to go in and share the gospel with this lady. She rolled her eyes and said "OK – I'll see you later."

So, I walked in, she greeted me and I said, "Ma'am, I don't know much about Christian Science (which was true). Would you be willing to tell me a bit about what you believe?" She replied that she would be delighted and spent ten minutes or so explaining all about Mary Baker Eddy and her book *Science and the Scriptures*.

I asked several questions because I really *was* interested in what she believed. Then I asked "Would it be OK if I shared with you some of the things I believe?" and she replied that she would be happy to listen. Then, I was able to explain about our sin debt, the biblical view of sickness and Jesus' offer of forgiveness.

If I had walked in there and started quoting the Bible and telling her that her beliefs were all wrong, she wouldn't have given me the time of day. And I wouldn't have blamed her a bit. But I treated her with respect; I listened to her first. I was genuinely interested in what she believed and I *earned the right* to share what I believed. Now, she didn't make a decision to trust in Jesus that day, but she clearly heard me.

A person can never 'unhear' something they have just heard

The words that people hear do register and they do go onto their hard drives. They may stay dormant for a long time, but God has the ability to use them in some very surprising ways. Let me give you an example of what God can do with just a small seed that you might plant with someone.

There is a young lady I have known for a long time but hadn't seen for several years. When I did see her again, I learned that she had become a mom – she had a 3-year-old son. While we were catching up with each other, one of the things I said to her was that my baby boy was in his thirties, but that I sure remembered those early days. Then I said this to her: "You know, one of the things I clearly remember about becoming a parent is that it really got me thinking more about spiritual things. How did it affect you?"

She replied "Oh, yeah – me, too. In fact, we go to church all the time." I asked where and she said she was attending a local non-denominational church. And then I said, "That sounds like a real good place. A lot of non-denominational churches talk about a personal relationship with Jesus. How about yours?" Her response was "They sure do. In fact, I just got saved last year." When

I said that I was so glad she had made that decision, she asked me "Do you know who got me thinking about spiritual things in the first place?" When I said I didn't, she looked at me and said, "*You* did."

Not only do I not remember what I said to her, I don't even remember saying anything spiritual to her at all. But obviously, God used a small seed that I planted in a very big way. So don't think that your words don't make an impact, because they do.

I also want to point out that the phrase I said to this young lady is a great one to use in many different situations. You can take this phrase, remove the part about becoming a parent and add something from your own life. "You know, one thing I clearly remember about…is that it really got me thinking a lot more about spiritual things. How did it affect you?" Come up with something that *did* impact you spiritually – something that matches what they're going through (a serious illness, losing a parent or a job, etc.). Because what they're experiencing just may be producing an open door in their heart.

Our lifestyle is very important, but a critical component of our witness is verbal

Have you ever heard the saying "Witness with your life and use words when necessary"? Well, I think that using words is *non-optional*. Is witnessing with your life necessary? Of course it is. Is it biblical? You bet it is. But the vast majority of the time, if people are going to understand the gospel message, someone is going to have to explain it to them *verbally*. Our lifestyle should compliment the message, but should never replace it. We can love and serve people in many different ways. But the most loving thing we can do for people is to explain spiritual truths to them in a way they can understand.

One of the best examples of a loving lifestyle along with a verbal explanation of the gospel is the account of Paul and the Philippian jailer. Paul could easily have taken the open cell doors as God's invitation for him to escape. But he knew that, if he did, the jailer would forfeit his life in the process. So Paul chose to remain in jail and save the life of the man who was his captor. Keep in mind that when Paul made this decision, he had no idea that the jailer would respond in any positive way at all. And when the jailer showed his openness to the good news, Paul gave one of the shortest explanations of the gospel in the New Testament: "believe in the Lord Jesus and you will be saved." (Acts 16:22-31) Paul's verbal explanation of the gospel was connected to his deeds. And since this jailer was no different than the people we relate to, we need to follow Paul's example.

We need to listen

If we don't listen to people first, we're not going to know what they don't know, what they need to hear, and what their misconceptions might be. We need to find out where the other person is spiritually. Once we know that, we can have a much better spiritual conversation with them.

So don't correct them or focus on what you're going to say next; just listen. This is definitely the hardest one for me. Those of us who are quick to correct others (like me) and quick to tell them what we believe (also like me) need to slow down, bite our tongues and *just listen*.

If we will just ask people in a gracious way what they believe, they will almost always tell us. And often, people believe what they believe for what they consider to be real good reasons. Those reasons may not make any sense to us but, to them, they can be very logical.

Suppose you find out that your friend is into Wicca or they worship some kind of nature god or they're into Eastern religion. Our first inclination is to want to correct them, right? Well, instead of doing that, try saying something like this: "It's great that you're into spirituality. Tell me more."

Wouldn't it be nice to use that phrase as our first response to people? No one wants to be immediately corrected when they have just shared something they really believe in. So try to put yourself in their place. Wouldn't you respond much better to someone who seems to be more interested in finding out what you believe than correcting you?

When you tell someone that you really want to know what they believe (and they sense that you mean it), it goes a long way. You will be surprised at how much people will share with you if you aren't being argumentative and self-righteous and if you're really interested. You'll also be surprised at how many arguments you can avoid this way.

Far too often, we make the huge mistake of jumping in too early and correcting people, which comes across as so self-righteous. When we approach people with the attitude that we know the truth (and they don't), and that we're here to correct them, I guarantee that we will turn them off and our spiritual conversations won't even get off the ground. Now obviously, for someone to start believing the truth, they have to stop believing what isn't true. So telling people what is true is important. But try to save that for a bit later in your conversations.

Another good way to avoid coming across as just another pushy, religious person is to ask for permission to talk about spiritual things. Yes, this does give the other person the chance to say 'no' and to prevent your spiritual conversation from ever starting in the first place. But doing this lets the other person know that you will respect their wishes and that you're not determined to tell them something, whether they want to hear it or not. Look at it this way: how do *you* typically respond when someone is pushy and overbearing with you? Do you want to talk with them or do you wish they would just go away?

Use some humor

A very important ingredient in our spiritual conversations is humor. Humor is always a great way to break the ice; it *always* reduces the tension with people. And let's face it: there is going to be some tension in these conversations. If we're not careful, our spiritual conversations can get way too serious way too quickly and the message will not come across clearly.

If you ask the average person to describe a spiritual conversation, they will probably use words like serious, scary, weird or boring. When we show people that it doesn't have to be that way, it really makes an impression on them. The last thing people expect from a 'religious' person is some humor and laughter. I assure you that if you use some humor with people, you will greatly reduce the tension that is so common in spiritual conversations. I can also tell you from experience that when you use some humor to lighten things up, the other person will be much more likely to talk with you about spiritual things.

For example, I know that you will run into many people who have some very negative perceptions of Christianity in general and of Christians in particular. And no matter what negative thing they say, you can respond with this: "You know, I heard a great little saying that I think you'll like. It goes something like this: One of the biggest barriers to people becoming believers in Jesus is the behavior of some of his followers."

Non-Christians *always* agree with this statement - and they usually laugh, too. Don't ever forget that many people got their negative perceptions from a real Christian who was being a lousy representative for Jesus. So do your best to not be one of them.

Follow God's leading

When you feel like God is leading you to a certain person or to say a certain thing, listen - because he may very well be. One of my favorite adjectives for God is 'sneaky' (in a good way, of course). He goes ahead of us and sets up situations that would be impossible for us to engineer. If we keep our eyes open, we will find him doing just that. But we have to be open to seeing them and we need to respond when one comes our way. I want to share one such situation with you.

I have a friend name Dave who went to high school with a lady who lives in Texas. She is also a believer in Jesus and sent my friend (who lives in Ohio) an email a couple of years ago about a man who had undergone a terrible tragedy. This man, who lived several hundred miles from where my friend lives, had been in a car accident (which was his fault) in which his only son had been killed. She asked Dave if he would contact this man and try to be of some comfort to him. But he came up with several good reasons not to: he didn't know him, he couldn't relate at all to what he had gone through, and he felt that it would be very awkward to just call him out of the blue. So he didn't.

Several months went by and this man kept coming to my friend's mind. Finally, he couldn't stand it any more and called him one evening. "My name is Dave, and we have never met. But I want you to know that a lot of people are praying for you." They went on to have a wonderful conversation, at the end of which the man prayed to put his faith in Jesus. Now, I would call that a divine appointment, wouldn't you? So listen to the promptings of the Holy Spirit, because they are real.

Ask for clarification

When someone makes a statement or asks a question, it's often helpful to ask them to restate it, just to make sure we understand what they really mean. How often have you assumed that you knew exactly what the other person was saying, but found out later that you were way off base? I have done this many, many times and on occasion still find myself doing it. You can simply say,

"What do you mean?" or "Tell me a bit more. I want to make sure I understand what you're saying."

A little illustration will help here. It's like the 10-year-old boy who comes into the kitchen and asks, "Mom, where did I come from?" Well, mom gives a big sigh, saying to herself "I knew this was coming, so now is as good a time as any." So, she gets out her 'materials' and has an extended talk with her son about the birds and the bees. Afterward, she looks at him and asks, "Now, do you have any questions?" He looks at her and says, "Yeah – Timmy said he came from Pittsburgh and I just wanted to know where I came from."

We may think we know what the other person is saying or asking, but it's wise to get more information and be completely sure. This is especially important in spiritual conversations, because people tend to have widely different definitions for 'religious' words. It's crucial to define our terms (and ask them to define theirs) if we're going to really communicate.

Agree with what you can

It's really hard to have an argument with someone who just agreed with you. And the best way to avoid getting into theological arguments with people is to go and 'sit on their side of the table'. When you start spiritual conversations with people, they will often bring up arguments and/or derogatory comments or they may just want to argue with you. When this happens, simply agree with what you can. For example, suppose that someone says to you "Those religious people are nothing but a bunch of hypocrites who want your money."

Instead of getting defensive (which is what I used to do), here's what I typically say: "You know, a lot of times, you're exactly right." Because you know what, folks? Unfortunately, far too often, they *are* exactly right. It's no wonder that so many people have negative views of Christians. I have found that there is always something that you can agree with, no matter what they say.

Here's something that you're sure to eventually hear: "How can there be only one way to God?" Or they may say, "You Christians are so arrogant. You think your way is the only right one." Again, an argument probably won't be very helpful. Instead, agree with what you can and say something like this: "You're right – that does sound arrogant. And I agree with you – nobody likes arrogant, narrow-minded people." We can all say that and mean it, right?

You could go on and say "But Christians didn't come up with that 'only one way to God' business – Jesus did. And if it isn't true that he's the only way we can have a relationship with God, it *is* incredibly arrogant and narrow-minded. But if Jesus is actually who he says he is, it isn't arrogant at all – it's just a statement of fact."

Find some common ground

People will always respond better to someone they have something in common with. Let's say you're from Dallas, Texas and you're a huge Cowboys fan. Suppose you're on a business trip to Europe and you're on a train and the person sitting across from you is wearing a Cowboys sweatshirt. I guarantee that you're going to have a conversation with that person. Why? Because you have something in common. But to use the common ground you have with people, you first have to find it. And the best way to do that is to *actively look for it*.

Here's a good example of using some common ground. I recently finished reading the Qur'an for the second time (in English, not in Arabic) – all 114 chapters – because I wanted to see for myself what it really says. I met a young man from a Muslim country in Africa and asked him if he had read the entire Qur'an and he said that he had read it several times. I told him that I had also read the whole book and he was shocked. I asked him how many Americans have told him that they have read it and he said "none."

Then I said I was shocked at how much we have in common since large portions of the Qur'an came directly from the Old Testament. We went on to have a wonderful spiritual conversation about the scriptures, the New Testament and even Jesus (with no arguments at all). If that surprises you, consider this: if someone from a Muslim culture said to you "I just finished reading the bible and was surprised to see how much we have in common", would you be open to having a spiritual conversation with that person?

"That may be..."

When we're sharing our faith in Jesus, one very important principle is that we want to win the person, not the argument. Well, some of us *do* love to win the argument. But that's not often how you win people, is it? The little phrase "that may be" is very helpful, especially when dealing with people who show up at your door

(Jehovah's Witnesses and Mormons). These folks are taught that they have *the* truth and you're not about to change their minds. And it's also good to use with people who just like to argue.

A Jehovah's Witness approached me in front of my house some years ago. I spent a few minutes listening to him and gladly accepted a copy of the Watchtower magazine. Then I told him I was confused and wondered if he could answer a question for me. This really made an impact on him because they *love* to answer your questions; they have an answer for every one of them.

So I asked him "How can God, who's perfect, let sinful people into his heaven?" He replied that he wasn't going to heaven and didn't even want to. As you can imagine, I was surprised and asked him why. His response was that Jehovah was going to fully restore the same planet we're standing on back to its original condition and that he was going to live forever right here.

Now, would it have been helpful for me to get into a long discussion with him about the end of human history? Of course not, because the real issue was whether or not this guy knew Jesus personally. So, I simply said "Well, that may be" (which completely avoided an argument). And then, I said "But it still doesn't explain how God is going to deal with our sins." At that point, I was able to explain the gospel very clearly to him and he listened. He listened because I didn't argue with him and because I showed him respect by first listening to what he had to tell me.

So when these folks show up at your door, don't simply close it and send them away. Talk to them – have a conversation and ask them some questions. Believe me, they will be much more likely to listen to what you have to say if you listen to them first. And you just may be able to plant a seed with them that will be the beginning of them leaving their false teachings behind and coming to faith in Jesus.

I have two friends who are very committed atheists. We have breakfast together every other week and talk for an hour or two. I think they have brought up every misconception and argument and reason not to believe that God exists. We have had some great discussions and I have shared a lot of spiritual truths with them. I know that we have avoided many, many arguments by me simply agreeing with part of what they say.

I certainly don't agree with their worldview, but we're friends and we enjoy each other's company. And I know that I'm showing them a believer in Jesus who isn't argumentative, defensive, uptight or self-righteous. Without this, we would never be able to spend the time together that we do. And I pray for them regularly, that God would take some of the things I have shared with them and produce some results some day.

Just be yourself

We shouldn't change our tone of voice or our personality when we talk about spiritual things. People expect us to get real weird when we bring up spiritual issues and it really surprises them when we don't.

Several years ago, I was having a conversation with a young lady who was real close to making the decision to trust in Jesus. She said that one of her biggest fears was becoming like "one of those people who never blink." I asked her what she meant and she said, "You know – those people who start talking about religion and get up in your face and their eyes get real big and they don't even blink." She was so turned off by these folks and she actually thought she would have to become one of them. And she was extremely relieved when I assured her that that's not a requirement. So just be yourself – God wants to use you just the way you are.

Watch for major changes in people's lives

When a person's life is interrupted by something major (good or bad), it often produces an open door for a spiritual conversation. A couple of years ago, I was walking around our neighborhood handing out flyers for a block party that we have every September. One of my neighbors was out in his driveway and we started talking. I knew his first name, but nothing else about him.

It turns out that he was a real talker and he shared with me that he was going through a very tough time. One of the things I said to him was "This may sound weird to you, but God really does exist. He really is there and he understands what you're going through." He looked at me and said "You're about the tenth person this week who's said that to me." I replied, "Well, maybe he's trying to get your attention." That opened the door for a really good spiritual conversation.

I'm sure you will interact with some military folks who have just returned from a tour of duty overseas. And many of them were risking their lives to be there. When I'm talking to someone who has just come back from a war zone, I always thank them for their service. And in the context of a conversation about their military service, it would sound very normal to say something like this: "You know, if I had been in harm's way like you were, I bet I would have been thinking a lot more about spiritual things. How did it affect you spiritually?" And they will probably tell you.

Actively look for common, ordinary things

You may not realize it yet (although I'm sure you're getting closer), but almost every conversation that we have contains numerous things that we can easily use to turn that conversation toward spiritual things in a very normal way. All you have to do is actively look for them. A good example is the conversation I had about the Tom Brady interview. I'm going to give you several more examples of very ordinary situations that led to real good spiritual conversations, simply because I was paying attention.

I have a friend who was diagnosed with a pretty severe case of multiple sclerosis and he knows that his condition is likely to be terminal. He knows that I'm a hospice volunteer and he mentioned that he would probably end up in hospice some day. In the context of this conversation, it was very natural for me to ask him "When you do die, do you know for sure where you're going to spend forever?" He gave the standard answer, which is "Heaven, I *hope.*"

So I said "If there were a way for you to know *for sure* that God would accept you, would you want to know what it is?" He replied, "Of course I would." So I asked him about his church background and found out that he attended a church frequently when he was growing up. I didn't have to spend much time on the bad news (his guilt), because he heard about that a lot growing up. But no one had ever explained grace to him – God's totally free gift for simply choosing to trust what Jesus did on the cross. Once he grasped what God's offer to him really was, he made the decision to trust Jesus.

I had a sleep study for apnea done at a local sleep clinic several years ago. And if you've ever had this done, you know the routine. They stick about a hundred wires on you, put you in a strange bed in a strange room and tell you to go to sleep. Since the young technician who was prepping me took about twenty minutes to complete his task, we had a chance to chat. It turns out that he was a skier, so we had something in common and he lived in a little town close by.

I commented that a friend of mine and I had ridden motorcycles through that area several times and we always stopped in the quaint little downtown area for a frozen yogurt. I said that it was amazing how many churches there were in that town – it seemed like there was one on every corner. He agreed and then I said that it probably got my attention because my friend and I go to "the same non-denominational church in the north end of town." I asked about his church background and he told me that he and his girlfriend sometimes go to a local Baptist church.

So I said, "My wife was raised in a Baptist church and I bet you probably hear them talk a lot about making a decision to trust Jesus." He replied, with obvious disinterest, "Yeah – every time we go." As he was finishing with me I asked him, "How about you? Have you ever made a decision to trust in Jesus?" He looked at me and said, "Nope." That was the end of our conversation, so I asked him if he would be there in the morning when I woke up. He said he would and that he would see me then.

In the morning, a different technician came in to free me from the wires and my new friend stuck his head in the door and said, "Hey, it was real good talking to you last night." I said that I had enjoyed it, too, and then I asked him "Are you planning to hit the slopes this season?" He said that he hoped to, to which I responded, "If you do, would you do me a favor?" He said "I guess so – what?" And I said, "Please don't go out there and get yourself killed before you make that decision to trust Jesus." He laughed, I laughed and then he was gone. And on occasion I still pray that God would water the little seeds I was able to plant with him.

My wife's mother lived for many years in Kentucky about two hours south of us, just across the Ohio River. One Friday, we were visiting her and I went to a local tire store to have some work done on my car. It was in the summer, so I was outside leaning against the building (which is what everyone there does). A guy about 20 feet from me (also leaning against the building) looked over and said hello. I responded and started chatting with him.

I mentioned that it was a Friday and asked him if he was on his lunch break from work. He replied that he was actually off on a disability from a recent accident. I asked about it and he gave me some details. Then, he said that he had been in several other wrecks before that, one of which was on a motorcycle. I said that he was lucky to still be alive and that God probably gave him another shot at life.

"Yeah, I think you're right" he replied. I told him that, with all of the foolish things that I did growing up, God had to be watching over me and that I thank him on a regular basis. I said, "In fact, I've been going to the same non-denominational church up in Columbus for many years." I asked him about his church background and I got to explain the gospel to him a couple of different ways. He had never had anyone explain God's offer in a way that made sense to him and I could tell that he really heard me.

I told him he could make the decision to put his faith in Jesus by himself, even in his truck on the way home, and that it would really change his life if he did. At that point, they called his name and he went inside to pay his bill. He went to his vehicle and started out of the parking lot. Then he stopped, got out and walked back over to me. He said "I want to thank you for explaining those things to me. I really appreciate it." I told him it had been my pleasure and I again encouraged him to make that decision. He left and I guess I'll have to wait until I get to heaven to see if he ever did.

Revisit previous conversations

One of the best ways to get better at turning your conversations in a spiritual direction is to revisit a previous conversation. Once you have a conversation with someone, you can always go *back* to that conversation and continue it without coming across as pushy or out of left field. When you first start trying to turn your conversations in a spiritual direction, there will be a lot of times when you just can't figure out a way to do it and still sound natural. And it will be really frustrating. And by the way, this still happens to me, too. Here's where remembering some of the details of your conversations will be important.

After the conversation is over, you can take the time to think about what they said. Then, you can go back to the person and say something like this: "You know, I've been thinking about something you said to me." And they will probably ask you what it is. Or, you can say, "You know, when we talked a couple of weeks ago, you told me…" Now, you're right back in the same conversation and you can say what you *wish* you had said the first time without sounding the least bit awkward.

I know that you have had conversations recently with people who aren't believers in Jesus. And I'll bet that now, you can remember something they said that you could have used to start a spiritual conversation. So now, you can go back and revisit your previous conversation without sounding the least bit out of place.

In order to revisit a previous conversation, though, you have to remember some of the things that the other person said to you. I strongly encourage you to do what I do after I speak with someone – *write the details down*. Then, you can take the time to think about what they told you and come up with something that you can use to go back and bring up spiritual things.

Mention something you've done to serve someone else

Have you donated any of your time to your church this past year? Have you participated in any of their ministries? Have you visited someone in the hospital or a nursing home? Have you helped with any of the children's programs or helped to serve food to the homeless? My real question is this: Have you done anything through your church this past year for someone who couldn't pay you back? If your answer is 'yes', then you know how rewarding it is to serve.

Let's say you're talking to someone who does volunteer work or is into serving other people in some way. You can say to them "Boy, that must really be rewarding." Now, *in that context*, it would sound very natural to say something like this: "You know, one of the most rewarding things I did last year was…" And you can mention that you did that very rewarding thing through the church that you attend. Then, it would be very natural to ask them about *their* church background and to begin a spiritual conversation.

In a conversation about serving people, I often say "You know, I think Jesus said it best – it'll make you happier to give than to receive." And then, it would be very natural to ask, "Haven't you found that to be true, too?"

When you share something that you've done for someone else or you do something nice for someone, people will often say, "That was really nice of you." And any time anyone says that to you, you can say this: "Thanks. But it's more than that – it's more than just being nice."

They will probably ask you what you mean and you can
say "Well, the truth is that God's been awfully good to
me and this is just one of the ways I can give some back."

You can say this anytime *anyone* compliments you
on *anything* nice that you've done. And after saying how
good God's been to you, this question would sound very
natural: "How about you – how has God treated *you*
lately?" You'll be surprised at how much people will tell
you if you just ask.

Speaking of doing something nice for someone, have
you ever done someone a favor and had them say "If I
can ever do anything for you, just let me know"? Well,
collecting on this offer can accomplish something real
strategic. I have a neighbor that I had been wanting to
come to a Bible study with me for quite a while. His
car was on the blink, so I took him to work a couple of
times. Afterward, he told me "If there's ever anything I
can do…" So, a week or so later, I said to him "Did you
mean it when you said to let you know if there's anything
you can do for me?" He replied "Absolutely."

So I said "Well, there is one thing." And, of course,
he asked what it was and I told him I would like for him
to come to a Bible study with me. I said, "I just want you
to come twice and check it out. You can ride with me and
I'll even buy you a cup of coffee and a doughnut." And he
did. Later, he thanked me for getting him to come and
told me how glad he was that I had been sneaky.

When it just doesn't work

Don't get the idea that these things I'm sharing with you always work for me, because they don't. I want to share a story with you about an encounter I had in Colorado several years ago. We had a family reunion and were staying at a hotel in a quaint little town in the Rocky Mountains.

On Saturday morning, as is my custom, I got up early and went for a walk, hoping to 'run into' someone to talk to. It was about 6:30 and no one was out, so I returned to the hotel and headed for the breakfast buffet. There was only one person there - a guy that I would guess was in his thirties. So we said hello to each other and I noticed that he was wearing a t-shirt with a motorcycle logo on it. Since I was a rider at the time, I asked what kind of bike he rode.

He told me and I asked if it would be OK to join him. We had some things in common and had a real good conversation. I found out a lot about him – where he lived, what he did for a living, what he was doing in Colorado, etc. We probably talked for 15 minutes and I was just getting ready to turn the conversation in a spiritual direction, when I felt a tap on my shoulder. It was a relative and he asked me "Do you mind if we join you?" As you can imagine, I wanted to say "No! Come back later!" I didn't, of course, so they sat down and put an end to my conversation with my new acquaintance. A few minutes later, he left and I never saw him again.

Afterward, I was so disappointed that I didn't get a chance to plant a spiritual seed. But then, I realized that

I could do something every bit as important. Maybe I couldn't talk to him about God, but I could certainly talk to *God* about *him*. Not only that, but every time I prepare to give my workshop, I think back and pray for him. I also ask everyone taking my workshop to pray for him. Now, I'm going to ask you to do the same. His name is Robert (don't worry about his last name – God knows who he is).

Please pray that God would put some followers of Jesus into his life and help him to really understand what God's offer is. Pray for a special work of the Holy Spirit in his heart. Earlier, I suggested that you make a written list of the people you're reaching out to, so that you can remember to pray for them. Because something we often forget is that it's every bit as important to talk to God about people as it is to talk to them about him.

When we get to heaven, wouldn't it be a joy to see Robert there and have him say to you "We never met, but the little prayer you said for me was one of the things that God used to get me here. Thank you so much."

Seven

Special Situations

This is a good place to mention some special situations that you'll probably encounter.

I don't want to hear it!

I have heard this on more than one occasion and if you haven't, I promise that you will. So, what do you do when someone looks at you and says this very bluntly? Well, you should honor their request. You should *temporarily* honor their request. You can always let some time go by and go back and say something like this: "I remember you saying you don't want to talk about anything spiritual. Do you still feel that way?" Or, you could say, "I remember you saying you don't want to talk about anything spiritual. I'll bet you have real good reasons for feeling that way. What are they?" And they just might tell you.

So if someone lets you know they're not interested, just let it go. Otherwise, you'll come across as another one of those pushy, religious people. Just remember that even though they're very closed today, that does not mean they will stay closed for the rest of their life.

Here's a little story about someone who started out really closed. Back in the nineties, I was very close to a lady who had no interest at all in spiritual things. And during the 3½ years we were together, I never did find out why. Tragically, she ended up dying of lung cancer in her late forties. She had two children in their teens, whose father had already died of cancer, and she desperately wanted to live to see them grow up. She was diagnosed in August and died one year later. I was with her through all of her chemotherapy and radiation, with still no interest in spiritual things.

Shortly after she accepted the fact that she was dying, she looked at me and said, "I've taken care of the lawyers and the guardian and the insurance policies. Is there anything I've missed?" I said, "Well, there is one little thing you need to consider." She asked what it was and I said, "You need to consider where you're going to spend forever." She replied "You've been trying to talk to me about this for three years. Now I'm going to listen."

Of course, I started with the bad news – that we're all guilty before God. She said "Believe me – I know I'm guilty." Then, I explained the simple gospel message – that she could have total forgiveness and a guaranteed place in heaven by deciding to put her faith and trust in Jesus and what he did on the cross. She looked at me and said "Now, you only have to do this *once?*" To which I replied, "Yes. If you really understand what you're doing, and you mean it, once will do." She said she would think about it. To make a long story short, she made that decision just a few weeks before her death.

The family members, most of whom had a very formal church background, asked me to say a few words at her funeral. I told a couple of funny stories about her and said, "The reason I can joke about her is that I know exactly where she is today." And then, I explained why. A lot of people heard the gospel message that day and I have prayed many times that God would water the seeds that were planted with them.

I have told her story to many people and each time, they clearly hear the gospel. Of course, as with all third party stories, I'm not talking *to them*; I'm talking *about her*. I have kept in touch with her daughter, who is now in her thirties, and I have talked to her several times about her mom and the decision she made. And I'm praying that someday she will understand God's offer and come to know him, too.

At times, it's OK to be extremely bold

We should never be pushy and overbearing, but there are occasions when we should be very bold. In 2 Corinthians 5:20, Paul was *begging* people to be reconciled to the Messiah. And sometimes it's appropriate for us to beg someone to respond to God's offer. It won't happen very often, but here's a situation where I did just that.

I got to spend a couple of hours every week for several months with an elderly gentleman who was dying of cancer. He had spent over 50 years studying with the Jehovah's Witnesses and he knew his Bible forward and backward. Well, let me put it this way – he knew the *content* very well. But he had no clue about a personal relationship with God and not a clue about who Jesus really is and what he came for, either.

The very first time I met him, he said to me "You know, Jeff, I'm not totally sure that Jehovah is going to accept me when I die." To which I replied, "Why don't we spend some time talking about that?" And we did. We spent many, many hours talking and I showed him numerous places in the Bible that prove that Jesus was far more than a good man. And I assured my friend that he could *know* that God would accept him simply by trusting Jesus personally. But he would have none of it. Many months later he was transferred from his brother's home to a VA medical facility to spend his last days.

One Saturday morning, I got up and thought "I think I'll go and see my friend today. " The clinic was about an hour away, and during the drive I was praying that God would open his eyes. When I got there and went into his room, it was obvious that he was actively dying, but he was glad to see me. I sat down by his bed, took his hand and said, "You know, you're going to meet Jesus face-to-face very soon. And when you do, he's going to look at you and say 'I don't know who you are'. I'm *begging* you to make the decision to trust him before it's too late. Let him into your heart and trust that his payment on that cross will pay for all of your sins." And he did. We prayed together and he asked Jesus to come into his life and have a relationship with him. Less than 24 hours later, he died.

God may provide you with a person who is very open to the gospel

Sometimes, when you least expect it, God will drop someone who's open right into your lap. One Friday night, I was going to meet a friend and do some target shooting. On the way there, I stopped at a local gas station and when I came out, a young lady in her early twenties approached me. It was pouring rain, she was soaking wet and she said to me "Sir, I have to get to the airport. Would you please give me a ride if I give you ten dollars?"

I replied that I would be happy to take her to the airport, but that I wouldn't take her money. That gas station is less than five minutes from the airport, so we had almost no time together. I found out that her name was Donna and I said "So, how is your life going, Donna?" And she told me – not very well.

So I simply asked "Have you ever considered letting God play a role in your life?" She replied, "I would love to. But how would I do that" So, I explained the bad news (no problem there) and the good news about trusting Jesus. We pulled up in front of the airport and she prayed and asked Jesus to come into her life. She thanked me, gave me a big hug and a kiss on the cheek and then she was gone. I never saw her again, but am looking forward to seeing her in heaven and having a good laugh about our brief time together.

On another occasion, I decided to go and visit a friend in the hospital one Sunday night. When I got there, he was talking with a young lady he knew from another group he was involved in. She asked me how we knew each other and I said, "We go to the same non-denominational church in the north end." So I asked about her church background and found out that she had been studying Buddhism for the past several years. But recently, she had said a prayer to the God she wasn't sure really existed that went something like this: "If you're really there, show me in a way I can't miss and I will respond."

The three of us had a long conversation about spirituality in general and Jesus (and who he claimed to be) in particular. At the end of that conversation, she made the decision to become a believer in Jesus. She shared with me a couple of years later that, during her initial prayer to God, she had also said something like this: "OK – if you're the real God, then here's what I want you to do. I want answers to these questions, but I'm not going to tell anyone what those questions are. If you're really God, this should be easy for you."

She told me that our conversation with her that night answered *every one* of those questions – questions that were known only to God. Coincidence? I don't think so. Obviously, God was working behind the scenes to set this whole thing up. But I want to point out that, even though she was very open to spiritual things, my friend and I both *chose* to open our mouths and share spiritual truths with her.

You will find open people in the most unlikely places

Let me put it this way: you'll find open people in the most unlikely places *if you're actively looking for them.* I had some pretty negative experiences in the dental chair growing up and, even though I'm a dentist, I don't go for a checkup nearly as often as I should. But one day, for some strange reason, I went to a friend's dental office for a checkup.

Now, if you've ever been to the dentist, you know how hard it is to have a real conversation with the hygienist, since she has her hands in your mouth most of the time. My friend's hygienist asked me how I knew her boss and I said that we "both go to the same non-denominational church in the north end of Columbus." So, of course, I asked about her church background and found out that she went to the same kind of church that I attended when I first moved to Ohio.

Very briefly (remember that she had an instrument in my mouth most of the time), I told her about my experiences in that church. And I shared with her that I never heard the minister talk about "personal salvation – you know, making a personal decision to trust Jesus. How do they present that at your church?" Well, as I suspected, they didn't. So I explained the gospel very simply and asked her if there was anything that would stop her from making that decision. She said there wasn't and, after she finished cleaning my teeth, she sat me up in the chair and prayed to trust Jesus.

So no matter where you find yourself in your daily life, assume that many of the people you talk to are spiritually open, because many of them really are.

Someone who is near the end of their life

Like with my older friend at the VA clinic, you may get the chance to spend time with someone in his situation. You will find that people at this stage of life aren't nearly as distracted as most of us are. They aren't at all concerned about a new house or a new car or the next vacation. And often this is when they're the most open to the gospel.

Several years ago, I got an email about a man in his forties who was in a nursing home and was dying of AIDS. I had never met him, but I volunteered to go and spend a couple of hours with him and see if I could make his life a little more comfortable. For whatever reason, his family rarely came to see him and he really appreciated anyone who would spend time with him.

When I introduced myself, I told him that I got his name from the hospice organization and that I was involved with several other hospice volunteers at "this non-denominational church I go to in the north end." A bit later, when I asked about his church background, he told me that he didn't have one at all. To which I replied "Lucky you." When he asked what I meant, I said, like I mentioned earlier in this book, "Well, just think of all the wrong stuff you don't have to unlearn." He thought that was hilarious.

We spent a couple of hours getting to know each other and I found out a lot of details about his life. He was a smoker and I wheeled him outside so he could smoke while we talked. He was literally just skin and bones at that point and was in chronic pain. But he asked me if I would rub his back, which he said really helped his discomfort. So, of course, I did - I tried my best to just make him comfortable.

Some time later, I said, "Even though you didn't grow up going to church, you've heard of Jesus, right?" He said "Oh sure." Then I said that a lot of people I've talked to, even those who *did* grow up going to church, don't really know what Jesus came to do. Then I said "You've heard the word 'gospel, right?" And then I explained the bad news (our sins). He had no problem admitting that he was far from good enough for God to accept him.

But when I explained that simply making a decision to trust Jesus based on what he did on the cross (once you believe that you really need it) was all he had to do, he said he was ready to do that. But, as I always do with someone who wants to pray, I stopped him. I always want to make sure that the person really understands what they're doing. And what I normally say to that person is this: A prayer won't make you God's adopted child; a *decision* will. That prayer is just your way of telling God that you're making a decision to trust Jesus." He did understand, and he prayed for Jesus' death on the cross to apply to him personally. A bit later, as I was leaving, I said, "You know, a thousand years from now, you'll be so glad that you made that decision." He looked at me and said, "Oh, believe me, I already am." And four days later, he died.

He had the opportunity to hear the gospel presented in a non-weird way (and just in time) because one of God's adopted children chose to speak up and explain it to him. Keep in mind that this book was written for the sole purpose of helping you to become more confident that you can do this, too, when the opportunity arises.

A very direct approach is sometimes appropriate

The better you know a person, the more direct (and sometimes even blunt) you can be without risking damage to your relationship. And this is true in every area – not just when you're talking about spiritual things. I had a close family member who was terminally ill, and his wife (also a very close family member) needed help getting him to the hospital for some outpatient surgery. So, I drove the three hours to their house on a Friday and planned to help her get him to and from the hospital on Monday morning. Then, I had planned to drive back home and run my office for the rest of the week.

He was a believer in Jesus, but his wife is one of the most closed people I have ever known to having a relationship with God through trusting in Jesus. And it's not for a lack of information – she has heard the gospel clearly explained dozens of times. She is rarely open to any kind of spiritual conversation. But as we were coming back from taking him to the hospital, something remotely spiritual came up, and she said to me, "I don't believe that a person can live their life doing bad things and then, at the end, be sorry and be forgiven."

I thought a lot about what she said and wondered how I might be able to respond to it. After much consideration (and prayer), I decided that what she really needed to hear was the parable that Jesus told about the landowner who hired workers all throughout the day and then gave them all the same wage (Matthew 20:1-16).

Due to some unexpected surgical complications, I ended up staying the whole week. The following Sunday morning, after he had come back from the hospital, I was getting ready to leave. She asked me if I wanted her to fix breakfast for me before I left, but I said that I needed to get back. Then, she made the huge mistake of asking "Is there anything I can do for you before you go?"

So, of course, I said, "Well, there is one thing." When she asked what it was, I said that I wanted to show her something in the Bible. She crossed her arms, leaned back in her chair, and said, "I don't want to hear it." So I crossed *my* arms and leaned back in *my* chair and said "I've been here helping you for ten days. I even closed my office for a whole week to do it. I think I've *earned* a few minutes of your time, don't you?" She thought for a minute and then replied, "Yeah, I guess you have."

I read that parable to her and said "Now, was it fair that the guy who only worked for ten minutes got the same pay as the guy who worked for eight hours? Of course not – it was way *better* than fair. And it's the same way with God's offer. Do we *deserve* to be forgiven? No, but we can have it for free if we'll just admit that we need it."

I don't know if any of the things I've said to her over the years have made a difference, but I do know that she has heard me. And since, like I mentioned before, a person can never 'unhear' something they've already heard, I believe that God will do something strategic in her life through the things she has heard from me and from many other people.

The other person may open the door for you

They may initiate a conversation with *you*, like the guy at the car service place did with me. Many years ago, I was in Portland, Oregon for a week for a seminar and, on Saturday morning, I went out for a walk to see the city. A young man about eleven or twelve approached me very nervously and asked if he could talk to me. I said, "Sure, I would be happy to talk with you." Now, this was on Saturday (the real Sabbath), he was carrying a bag over his shoulder and he had a handful of magazines. Can you guess who he was? Right – he was a Jehovah's Witness.

I listened to what he had to say and gladly accepted a copy of the Watchtower magazine. And then I said "Would it be OK if I share with you a little of what I believe?" He said "Sure", so I explained my faith in Jesus and that he also could have total forgiveness by trusting him personally. He obviously had never had anyone explain grace to him and he listened very intently. A minute later, his mom came around the corner with a toddler in tow. When she heard me talking to him about faith in Jesus, she snatched him away as quickly as she could.

As she was leading him away from me down the street, he turned and looked at me. I smiled and waved and silently mouthed the words "I'll pray for you." He smiled back and then they were gone. Who knows what God did with the small seeds I planted with that young boy. But again, I know that he heard me and that somehow that young man's life is a little different because of our conversation.

Sharing the gospel can really impact someone who's already a Christian

I have already mentioned it, but I practice dentistry for a living. And at my office, like at most dental offices, sales people often show up unannounced. I rarely have time to talk to them and, to be honest, I usually just have my assistant talk to them even if I do have some time.

But on one occasion, many years ago, my staff and I were standing at the counter in the business office at the end of the day. We had finished seeing our patients and two salesmen walked in and asked my assistant if they could talk to me. Like I said, normally she would say no. But for some reason, I asked her to have them come in. I introduced myself and we went into my office and sat down.

They were trying to convince me to start selling their

products to my patients and I politely listened to their presentation. When they were finished, I told them I wasn't interested, thanked them for coming and thought they would just let it go. But, being good salesmen, they tried again to convince me. One of them was about my age (I was in my early thirties at the time) and the other was about fifteen years older. The younger one told me that I could fund my entire retirement with the profits I could make.

I responded that my retirement was already taken care of and he asked "How did you manage to do that at your age?" I said, "Oh – you mean *that* retirement. I'm talking about my *real* retirement. I'm a believer in Jesus and I know for sure where I'm going to spend forever. That's the best retirement of all." They looked at me, then looked at each other, thanked me for my time and got up and left.

A few minutes later, the older man came back in and asked if he could talk to me. I said, "Sure – come on in" and we went back to my office. He looked at me and said "I've been a believer in Jesus for many years and I've been very hesitant to share my faith. But the fact that you didn't know us from Adam, yet you were willing to talk about Jesus, is going to change that for me. I'm going to leave here and start sharing my faith a lot more often."

What I did that day was a very small thing, but it may turn out to have been very significant. I can't wait to see some of the people who were impacted by this man's change in attitude when I get to heaven. Your spiritual conversations with people who already know Jesus personally may be just the thing that motivates them to go out and share their faith, too. And someday, you will be able to see just how significant those seemingly minor things that you did and said really were.

EIGHT

"I JUST DON'T BELIEVE IT"

No book on sharing your faith would be complete without a chapter on the objections to faith that we hear from people so often. Since God has given each of us true free will, it means that we can choose to deny what, deep down inside, we know is really true (Romans 1:18-20). So when someone brings up an objection to belief in the existence of God or the reality of Jesus' death and resurrection, I look at it as an opportunity. When a person is willing to discuss spiritual things, even when they adamantly deny that they're true, we have an opportunity to plant a seed in their minds that will never go away. And if you think about it, when someone brings up an objection, or even starts an argument with you, what they're really doing is simply extending the spiritual conversation.

And isn't that what we want to happen? We all know that we can't argue someone into God's family. And I hope you realize that you can't convince someone of the reality of biblical truth; only God's Spirit can do that. All we're called to do is to be God's ambassadors and his messengers. When you share biblical truth with another person, you are planting a seed in their minds that God may eventually use in a strategic way in their life. Whether or not they believe what you're saying is completely immaterial. So the next time someone gives you a reason why they don't believe what you believe, be glad. Not only are they extending the conversation, they are also giving you another opportunity to go a little deeper into what they believe. And the more you know about where someone is spiritually, the more effective you can be in asking questions that will make them think.

Any time someone brings up an objection, just like when they ask a question, we should make sure we understand what they're saying before we respond. It's always appropriate to ask, "What do you mean?" and give them a chance to flesh out their statement a bit. Often, we'll find that there is much more to their objection than the simple statement that they just made. Adding a question like "Why do you say that?" or "Why do you feel that way" might be helpful, too.

One of our goals is to try to find out not only what the other person believes, but also *why they believe it*. If we can get below the surface of someone's question or statement or objection, and find out the belief behind their words, we can have a much better conversation. Open-ended questions (after which we really *listen*) are the best way to accomplish this.

For example, suppose you have gotten spiritual things out on the table and you have shared some biblical truth and the other person says, "I don't believe any of that stuff." One response, the one we would often *like* to give them, would be to say "Why not? It's true" (which will always produce an argument). How different that is to simply asking ""Why not?" or "Why do you feel that way?" Their answers to these questions will get you a lot closer to their real problem with spiritual things.

Suppose the person says to you that they don't believe
any of that stuff and you ask them why. There are dozens
of reasons why a person would say something like that.
They may say "I heard way too much of that stuff growing up," to which you might reply: "What was it that
bothered you about the things you heard?" They may
say, "It wasn't so much what they said, but the way they
said it." Again, you might just ask, "What do you mean?"
They might reply: "Well, they always came across like
they were better than everyone else. And they said one
thing on Sunday, but acted a lot differently when they
were outside the church." You could then say, "I bet that
really turned you off," to which they may reply, "You
have no idea."

Now you know the real reason they said that they
weren't interested: hypocrisy. If you had responded to
their initial statement before asking some questions, you
would have never known why they said what they did.
But now, you can say something like this: "Boy, I don't
blame you a bit for not being interested. If I had had
those experiences, I would probably feel the same way."
At this point, you are 'on their side' and you understand
why they feel the way they do. Put yourself in their place:
wouldn't you tend to respond that way if that had been
your experience growing up? Always look for an opportunity to get past a person's initial objection and try to
find out the real feelings behind it. Then, you can address
the real issue behind their words.

"I'm glad you found something that works for you"

One of the best ways to deflect biblical truth is to play the 'all opinions are equally valid' card. What they're saying is that your opinion is right for you, but that theirs is just as right for them. When we hear something like this, our first reaction is to insist that our beliefs are also true for them. Since that won't even make a dent in their opinion, a better response would be to say: "What do you mean 'works for me'?" They will very likely respond with "Well, what you believe makes you a better person" or "Your beliefs make your life better." And if you think about it, truer words were never spoken. Your belief in Jesus *does* make you a better person , and it definitely makes your life better.

I suggest you agree with them and say, "You're absolutely right. It does make my life better (or it does make me a better person)"? And then, you can follow that with "I'm curious. What makes *your* life better?" or "What makes *you* a better person?" If you really listen to what they tell you, you will very likely be able to agree and say something like "I'm sure that *does* work for you."

Then you could say something very true that they will almost always agree with: "Well, if your goal is to simply be a better person (or to live a better life), almost all belief systems will do that. You've just found the one that's the most comfortable for you, right?" You'll notice that there hasn't even been the hint of an argument in this conversation. And it's because you've chosen to really listen to them and to agree with what you can. If you follow these two principles, you will be shocked at how often you can have a conversation with someone who disagrees with almost everything you believe, yet have a better relationship with them afterward. And that's one of our biggest goals: to build relationships with people who are far away from God. And if your conversation has gone this far, it may be appropriate to add this: "But if your goal is to have your sins forgiven, there's only one way to do that. And that is to find out what God says about how that can happen."

"That's just your opinion"

This is similar to the previous objection, but in this case the other person isn't insisting that their views are equally valid. They're just saying that your worldview is simply an opinion. To this, I would respond "You're right; it is my opinion. But an opinion can reflect something that's actually true." At this point, they may say the same thing that Pontius Pilate asked Jesus: "What is truth?" (John 18:38). Here is the approach that I might use in this situation:

> "Let me ask you a question. What's your favorite flavor of ice cream? OK – you're absolutely convinced that chocolate is the best one. What if I say that vanilla is much better? You have one opinion and I have another and they're completely different. But we're both right, because flavors of ice cream don't reflect any kind of objective truth. And in the big scheme of things, ice cream preferences don't matter at all, do they?

"But suppose you're at the airport waiting to board
a flight and the passengers who just arrived are
getting off the plane that you're going to get on.
And the last passenger to leave the plane loudly
announces to everyone: 'Don't even think about
getting on this plane! I'm an aeronautical engineer
and I help design these things. I heard a noise that
I'm real familiar with and it was a major failure in
one of the control systems. This plane needs to
be taken out of service or some people are going
to die.'"

After hearing this, you would probably approach the
ticket agents and express your concern. What if they said,
"That guy flies with us all the time and he routinely says
those things. He's just a nut job." Now, their opinion is
that the plane is perfectly safe. But the other guy's opinion
is that the plane is very likely to crash. They can't both
be right, can they? One opinion is right and one is wrong.
And does it matter? You bet it does. Well, either God
really exists or he doesn't. And if he does, and if how we
relate to him is going to affect where we spend eternity,
that matters a great deal, too.

I have known a man for several decades who has
one of the best defenses to spiritual truth that I have
ever heard. He simply answers every spiritual question
with "I don't know." For example, I have asked him if he
believes that God exists. His answer is that he doesn't
know. When asked if he thinks this incredibly complex
universe simply appeared by accident out of nowhere, he
says he doesn't know. When asked what he believes about
spiritual things, he simply says, "I really don't know what

I believe." If his goal is to frustrate me (or anyone else who's trying to have a spiritual conversation with him), he has succeeded. The last time I brought up spiritual things, I left him with this statement: "Well, one of two things is definitely true here. Either I'm wasting my life serving a God who doesn't exist, or you're wasting your life ignoring the God who does exist." It didn't change his mind, but I know that he did hear me and that he will never forget what I said.

One of the most effective things that you can do with a person whose beliefs are light years away from biblical ones is to try to graciously poke a hole in their worldview. And any worldview that doesn't include a belief in God is easy to poke holes in. As I mentioned earlier, I have two friends who are both very committed atheists that I have been building a relationship with for several years. We have been meeting for breakfast every other week for two hours and have discussed spiritual things many times. They know exactly where I'm coming from and what I believe and they have heard the gospel explained many different times in many different ways. They have said some of the most insulting things imaginable about the God that I believe in. And they also never hesitate to say that people who believe in anything religious are extremely ignorant. If I had let any of their comments offend me, I would have missed the opportunity to poke several huge holes in their worldview.

Now, keep in mind that I know these guys. We have a good relationship, which means that I can say some things to them that I might not say to a casual acquaintance. One of the things I have said to them is to point out that their atheism, just like my belief that God does exist, is a faith position. If someone says to you "You can't prove that God exists," you can respond with "And you can't prove that he doesn't." I have also pointed out to them that if they actually believe that the universe just happened out of nothing, without an intelligent cause, they have much more faith than I will ever have.

Another thing I have pointed out to them is that if their worldview is true, if we are all just a collection of random molecules and electrical impulses, their family members are no more valuable than a rat. One of them has several children and, when asked if he loves them, he will say that he does. I can point out that his statement presents a problem: if his worldview is correct, there's no such thing as love; we're simply wired by our environment and our electrical connections to respond to a certain stimulus a certain way. He may say that he agrees with me, but you and I know that he (and every other atheist) doesn't live this way. In fact, they all pretend that love exists, that certain things are objectively wrong, and that people do matter (especially the ones in their families). Atheism is the easiest worldview to poke holes in because no one can even come close to living consistently with it.

"You're a person of faith, but I'm a person of facts (or science)."

Finally, a lot of people want to make a distinction between fact and faith. They see faith as a blind leap in the dark that weak people use as a crutch to get them through life. They also tend to see faith as choosing to believe something that you know in your mind isn't true. But the real definition of faith is this: an informed decision to believe something that can't be scientifically proven based on what you consider to be good evidence. We can point out that most of life (for them as well as for us) is lived by faith. In fact, every one of us bets our life on certain things we simply take by faith. Every time you get into your car, you have faith that the brakes are going to work properly, even though you haven't disassembled the system to check it. Every time you drive across a bridge, you have faith that the bridge will safely support you. You simply have faith that the bridge is safe, based on the fact that it's still standing. Many years ago in West Virginia, people were in their cars on the Silver Bridge and all of them had faith that the bridge would safely support them. Unfortunately it collapsed, killing many of those people.

Whether or not we live by faith isn't the issue at all, because everyone does it every day. The real issue is what we base our faith on. There is a very popular false dichotomy between science and religion that almost all atheists refer to. They dismiss the idea of a personal God because many, like my two friends, simply don't want to believe that he exists. They are, as Romans 1:18 says, willfully suppressing the truth. No amount of logical arguments can change the mind of someone who has decided ahead of time that God is simply a figment of our imagination.

So hang in there with your friends who are atheists and agnostics, even the ones who are very hostile and insulting toward God. Also, pray for them on a regular

basis. Have friendly discussions with them without getting offended and argumentative. Plant seeds in a gracious
way and become their friend, because you may be the only
believer in Jesus that they associate with. And if a door
ever opens in their heart, you may be the one person that
God can use to reach them with the gospel.

Conclusion

The kinds of situations I have described in this book happen in my life all the time. But it's not because there's anything special about me. Granted, I've been doing it for a long time. But these things happen because I'm *actively looking* for ways to bring up spiritual things in my normal, everyday conversations. I'm also thinking along certain lines and trusting that God will open doors. And when I find an opening, I consciously choose to pursue it, despite the fact that I continue to feel a bit nervous doing so.

The bottom line is really this: if you actively look for ways to turn your conversations in a spiritual direction, you will find them. And once you get to the point where you think this way, you won't have to force yourself to have spiritual conversations – they will come very naturally.

At this point in my life, I often have to force myself *not* to have a spiritual conversation with someone. Now, I didn't develop this mindset in a month or two. It took some time and effort. But if you start changing the way you think, you'll be surprised how quickly you'll get to this same point, too.

As has been said a couple of times, talking to God about unsaved people is a critical component of being an effective sharer of your faith. When you're going to turn a conversation in a spiritual direction, silently ask God to use his Spirit in the other person's heart. Then, choose to believe that he's doing so as you speak with them. Start your day by reading those passages in Colossians 4 and pray that God would use you that day to plant a spiritual seed with someone that you are going to interact with.

I've given you a lot of things to think about in this book. And you may be thinking at this point that you will never be able to do these things on the fly – while you're in the middle of a normal, everyday conversation. If that's how you feel, don't get discouraged. Because guess what? You don't have to. Like I said, the very best way to develop skills in this area is to *go back* to a previous conversation that you have had with someone.

Start really listening to the things that people tell you and start writing them down. Then take the time to think about what they said. I promise you that, if you do this, you will always find something they said that you can use to turn the conversation around without being pushy or awkward. Then go back and revisit something they said to you. The more you do this, the easier it will get and the more natural it will feel. And your spiritual conversations will be much less stressful, both for you and your friend.

Finally, I want to urge you to make it a personal goal to help encourage someone else to get excited about sharing his or her faith. This may be one of the most significant things you can do. For many years, I thought that if I spent the majority of my time sharing the gospel that my life would impact the most people. But I came to realize that it's equally important to help others catch this vision, because you never know the impact that *they* are going to have.

Many years ago, a young man came to know Jesus personally, and an older man encouraged him to go out and share his faith with people. The older man probably thought that what he did was a very small thing. And it was – at the time. But he had no idea what that small encouragement would lead to, because that young man's name was Billy Graham.

We can have a huge impact on the world by simply helping some other people get more excited and better equipped to go out and do the most important thing in the universe – to share the good news about Jesus.

Thank you so much for investing the time to read this book. If you have any suggestions as to how I can improve the material I've presented here, please send me an email. And if your church would like for me to come and present my workshop in person, feel free to contact me.

My email address is:

jeff@initiatingspiritualconversations.com

RECOMMENDED BOOKS ON SHARING YOUR FAITH

One Thing You Can't Do In Heaven by Mark Cahill
    The author has personally witnessed to hundreds of people and has some very interesting stories. He has some very creative ways of starting and having spiritual conversations with people that he doesn't personally know and he uses a lot of printed materials. Some of his methods may not fit your style of sharing your faith, but this book is well worth reading. If you want to read one book by someone who is totally committed to evangelism, this is the one.

Out Of The Salt Shaker by Rebecca Pippert
    Although this book was written decades ago, it is a must read for anyone wanting to see good examples of 'lifestyle evangelism'. Pippert spends a good bit of time on the biblical basis for developing relationships and what living a committed life looks like to a watching world. She tells some fascinating stories of very unlikely people coming to know Jesus.

Share Jesus Without Fear by Bill Fay
    Bill Fay has a unique approach, which he has used to personally share the gospel with thousands of people. He asks a series of five questions (which you can adapt to suit your own style) and then has the person read selected

verses from the Bible and tell what they mean to them. It's a very non-confrontational method of sharing the gospel that you may find very comfortable using.

Walk Across The Room by Bill Hybels

The author (a founder of Willow Creek Church near Chicago) has a real heart for serving people. He spends most of the book encouraging us to come alongside people who don't know Jesus and, over a period of time, be a 'resource provider' for them. It is in this context that he tries to move them slowly toward faith in Jesus. This book was written by a man who really loves people.

Witnessing Without Fear by Bill Bright

Bill Bright is the founder of Campus Crusade for Christ. His book contains many interesting witnessing stories and is well worth the time it takes to read. He is also the author of the booklet 'The 4 Spiritual Laws' and highly recommends using it. For those of you who want to use printed materials in your witnessing, this might be a good choice for you. Especially good is his treatment of people who respond to the gospel with hostility, whom he challenges with a '30 day experiment.' He also includes a very good section on follow-up for the new believer.

YouTube videos of Walter Martin (search for 'Walter Martin and Jehovah's Witnesses')

Although he died in the late 80's, there are many excellent presentations on YouTube by Dr. Walter Martin, who was *the* expert on witnessing to cult members for many years. He gives a lot of very practical tips on how to plant seeds of doubt with those sincere, but misguided, people who often show up at your door. Highly recommended for anyone who wants to be able to share Jesus with people who are caught up in the cults.

God Space by Doug Pollock

Doug Pollock is the evangelism trainer for Athletes In Action and has had spiritual conversations with people all over the world. His main focus is trying to establish a safe place for non-believers to share what they think about God and Christianity and then to move them a step in God's direction. He is especially good at drawing out what people believe and why they believe it. Meeting people "where they are instead of where we would like for them to be" is the main focus of his book. His main tools are listening, noticing, and wondering, and he is very effective in using these to enter into conversations with people who are often very far from God.

Doug has a whole chapter in his book on the top 10 things Christians often do to kill spiritual conversations. If you go to his website GodsGPS.com, you can read chapter two online.

Becoming a Contagious Christian by Bill Hybels and Mark Mittleberg

I especially recommend reading chapter 9, which contains six different approaches to dealing with people. These six descriptions are based on people in the New Testament whose approach to sharing their faith flowed from simply being themselves. If you feel that your temperament or personality disqualify you from being an effective sharer of the good news, this is a must read for you.

"And *pray* for us, too, that God may *open a door* for our message, so that we may *proclaim the mystery of Christ*, for which I am in chains. Pray that I may proclaim it *clearly*, as I should. *Be wise* in the way you act toward outsiders; make the most of *every opportunity*. Let your conversation be always full of *grace*, seasoned with salt, *so that you may know* how to answer everyone."

(Colossians 4:3–6)